Mastering the Sicilian

Danny Kopec

May, 2001

To Ross & Harvey

With Many Thanks
and Best Sicilian
Wishes,
Danny

B.T. Batsford Ltd, *London*

First published in 2001
© Danny Kopec 2001

ISBN 0 7134 8482 9

British Library Cataloguing-in-Publication Data.
A catalogue record for this book is
available from the British Library.

Printed in Great Britain by
Creative Print and Design (Wales), Ebbw Vale
for the publishers,
B.T. Batsford Ltd,
9 Blenheim Court,
Brewery Road,
London N7 9NT

A member of the Chrysalis Group plc

A BATSFORD CHESS BOOK

Contents

	Page
Dedications and Acknowledgements	4
Background; Who is this book for?	5
1 The Scheveningen Structure	10
2 The Dragon Structure	33
3 The Richter-Rauzer Variation	56
4 The Characteristic Boleslavsky Structure	76
The Najdorf Variation	77
The Boleslavsky Variation	91
5 The Kan Structure and its Relatives	97
The Kan Variation	97
The Taimanov Variation	102
6 Offbeat Systems and a Repertoire	107
7 Closed Systems	110
The Closed Sicilian	111
The Grand Prix Attack	121
The c3 Sicilian Variation	123
The Kopec System	124
Closed Systems with ♗b5	126
Index of Games	128

Dedication & Acknowledgements

I would like to dedicate this book to my cousin Joseph Donath who taught me how to play chess and how to counterpunch, which is an essential skill for any successful practitioner of the Sicilian Defence. I would equally like to thank my wife Sylvia and son David for tolerating me during the process of writing this book. Acknowledgements are also due to my best friend, Dr. Daniel Reinharth, for proofreading the manuscript, my longtime friend Hal Terrie for technical assistance and FM Rudy Blumenfeld for additional help.

Last but not least, I would like to thank my friend and commissioning editor for Batsford, GM Nigel Davies, for his persistence in getting me to complete this work.

Finally, I would like to thank all those who have encouraged my chess activities over the years.

Reference Material

Batsford Chess Openings 2 by Garry Kasparov and Raymond Keene.
Encyclopedia of Chess Openings, Vol B (II) Ed. Aleksandr Matanovic
Fischer vs. Spassky: The Chess Match of the Century by Svetozar Gligoric
Best Chess Games 1970-1980 by Jon Speelman
Best Games of the Young Grandmasters by Craig Pritchett and Danny Kopec
Kasparov v Short 1993 by Raymond Keene
Kasparov's Opening Repertoire by Leonid Shamkovich and Eric Schiller
Kasparov is still the Man article in *Inside Chess* by Yasser Seirawan
Mastering the Nimzo-Indian by Tony Kosten
My 60 Memorable Games by Bobby Fischer
Practical Middlegame Techniques by Dr. Danny Kopec
The Sicilian: An Overview by Jon Edwards with contributions by Ron Henley
Sicilian Lines with e5 by T.D. Harding and P.R. Markland
Bobby Fischer's Chess Games, Eds. Robert Wade and Kevin O'Connell

Databases

The Ultimate Game Collection, Chess-4-Less, Inc., 1 million games from 1485-1997
Master Chess 2000, Chess-4-Less, Inc., over 1 million games from 1485-2000

Background: Who is this book for?

This book is intended for the player who wishes to develop a good understanding of the most important systems in the Sicilian Defence. It is not a book which attempts to cover all lines or variations—or even the most current ones. My goal has been to show the main formations (patterns) and themes which can arise in different Sicilian variations. The book is written distinctly from *Black's point of view* and designed to provide an inherently sound and viable opening repertoire. Pawn structures, typically arising from these systems, will be presented and discussed. I am not interested in asking the reader to memorize lots of moves and long, deep variations. This has never been my approach to chess and I don't advocate it. I would much rather the reader becomes familiar with frequently occurring and important themes in any system which he/she may wish to adopt as Black.

For many years I have believed that the difference between a strong club player and an expert, master and beyond, is the ability to recognize, strive for, and exploit the appropriate *levers* in a position. A lever is a pawn move which (1) offers a trade and (2) improves the lever-playing side's pawn structure and/or damages the opponent's pawn structure. In many examples I will take the reader to the point where appropriate levers have been achieved and Black's further play is clear. Understanding the levers in a position will help you to determine where the various pieces should go.

Some players would like an all-purpose formula to handle the opening. There is of course no such thing. However, if you are familiar with structures, methods of development and positional and tactical motifs, you will go a long way towards feeling confident when playing the Sicilian Defence.

Most games presented with each Sicilian opening system will be prefaced by a "Mastery Lesson", designed to summarize the important features of the game, particularly from Black's perspective, in terms of goals, motifs, and achievements. This is a rather original approach and will give the reader a unique opportunity to come away from each game with heightened knowledge and understanding, which in turn should make for increased playing strength. However, a word of caution. I do not think that readers who are unaware of the importance of rapid piece development and king security and who are still making basic tactical errors, are really ready for this book.

The Sicilian is generally accepted as the most popular defence for Black. One might well ask why it has been the preferred choice for tournament players at every level? I contend that there are three primary reasons:

(1) The opening offers Black excellent chances for counterplay from double-edged positions.

(2) There are a variety of systems, both solid and complex, from which Black can choose.

(3) The opening and a number of its primary systems lead to pawn structures which inherently favour Black, both in the middlegame and ensuing endings.

Let me briefly elaborate on each of these points.

Counterplay

The asymmetric first few moves lead to Black's enjoying a "span" of six squares on the half-open c-file, obtained after 1 e4 c5 2 ♘f3 d6 (or ...♘c6, or ...e6) 3 d4 cxd4 4 ♘xd4 etc., to White's span of five on the half-open d-file (after Black plays ...d6). This means Black will have considerable queenside counterplay, frequently associated with the advance ...b5. I have often been surprised to find how easily Black's game plays itself after he reaches the middlegame. Common targets are White's pseudo-backward pawn on c2 and the white pawn on e4 which in Open Sicilian variations (our primary concern) often lack defence from other pawns. Perhaps the reason that the Sicilian, more than other opening, leads to such ready

counterplay for Black is that the goals of the two sides are so distinct and different. Typically, the first sign of achievement for Black is the gaining of queenside counterplay and space by ...b5. The culmination of successful queenside play may manifest itself in control of the entire queenside or about a third of the board. This may then be followed by Black taking control of the centre —which in fact he contests from the very first move. Finally, play might shift to a direct assault on the white king, resulting in total victory. In an ideal situation, Black will gain control of at least three quarters of the board.

Complexity

The tension created by Black's flexible central structure (with pawns on d6 and e6 for example) against White's central e4/f4 pawn duo (sometimes enhanced with a pawn on g4), with possible conversion to a kingside attack, is why the Sicilian Defence leads to such complex play. This tension is further increased if White castles queenside and Black castles on the other wing. Black's pawn structure is inherently sound and can be tolerated even when he plays ...d6 and ...e5 (the Boleslavsky Structure). The latent possibility of playing ...d5 and/or ...e5, as may be the case, is the source of the tension I am referring to. This inevitably leads to very complex play. Furthermore, exchanges do not necessarily relieve the tension from White's point of view since his attacking chances are then likely to be reduced. Turning to an example from practical play, there is no better way of appreciating the positive features of the Sicilian Defence than by looking at a logical and indeed model game by the great Bobby Fischer.

M.Matulović-R.Fischer
Vinkovci 1968

1 e4 c5 2 ♘f3 d6 3 d4 cxd4 4 ♘xd4 ♘f6 5 ♘c3 a6 6 g3
White's choice is rather unusual and allows Fischer to react in a very active way.
6...e5 7 ♘de2 ♗e7

8 ♗g5
The struggle for control of the d5 square begins. Had White played the more routine ♗g2, then play would most likely have continued 8...0-0 9 0-0 b5 10 a3 ♘bd7 11 ♗e3 ♕c7, followed by ...♖ac8, ...♖ad8, ...♗b7, and ...♘b6 as necessary.
8...♘bd7 9 ♗h3
White tries to find real activity for his bishop but in view of the bishop's subsequent retreat, the text appears to be flawed.
9...b5
Fischer actively engages in the struggle for control of d5. Matulović-Minić, Belgrade, 1965,

went 9 ....0-0 10 a4! h6 11 ♗xf6 ♘xf6 12 ♗xc8 leaving White with the better game.
10 a4?
Here, this move does not fit into White's plans as Black gains control of the c-file—thanks to a very original idea by Fischer.
10...b4 11 ♘d5 ♘xd5 12 ♕xd5 ♖b8 13 ♗xe7

13...♔xe7!
And this is it! Fischer demonstrates his deep appreciation of the position. Now he quickly emerges with classic counterplay on the c-file.
14 ♕d2 ♘f6 15 ♗g2
Matulović correctly refrains from the exchange of his light-squared bishop so as to leave himself with chances of contesting the light squares. However, his position now becomes passive as a result of some incisive play by Black.
15...♗b7 16 ♕d3 ♕b6 17 0-0 a5
Now ...♗a6 is a real threat and White is struggling to survive. It is amazing how effective Fischer's opening play—spearheaded by the recapture 13...♔xe7!—has proved itself to be.
18 ♖fd1 ♗a6 19 ♕d2 ♖hc8 20 h3 h5

Here we see that kind of domination in board space that I mentioned earlier.

21 b3

To stop ...♖c4, but Fischer immediately recognizes the possibility of creating a good knight against a bad bishop.

21...♗xe2 22 ♕xe2 ♖c3 23 ♖d3 ♖bc8 24 ♖xc3 ♖xc3 25 ♔h2 ♕c5

The pressure on the backward c-pawn mounts. It is safe to say that already White has a lost game. 26 ♖c1? loses to 26...♖xb3.

26 ♖a2 g6 27 ♗f1 ♕d4

The shift to the domination of the centre begins.

28 f3 ♖e3 29 ♕g2 ♕d1

Black now controls the entire queenside and centre. About three-quarters of the board in fact! The time has almost come for White to resign.

30 ♗c4 ♕xf3 31 ♕xf3 ♖xf3

Here comes the famous Fischer technique—but even lesser players could win from here.

32 ♔g2 ♖e3 33 ♗d3 ♘xe4 34 ♗xe4 ♖xe4 35 ♔f2 d5 36 ♖a1 d4 37 ♖d1 ♖e3 38 h4 ♖c3 39 ♖d2 ♔e6 40 ♔g2 f5 0-1

Superior Pawn Structure for Black

As outlined in the discussion which follows, I truly believe that the Sicilian Defence offers Black a pawn structure which is sounder than White's. The potential of Black's two central pawns, in contrast to White's single central e-pawn, and the ease with which Black can maintain or try to improve his structure, particularly in the Scheveningen and Dragon Systems, implies that his pawn structure is inherently sounder and more dynamic than his opponent's.

My purpose here is to cover the following Sicilian pawn structures (systems) and the opening play which is integral to them:

(1)	**The Scheveningen pawn structures**
(2)	**The Dragon structure**
(3)	**The Rauzer Variation**
(4)	**The Paulsen or Boleslavsky pawn structures**
(4a)	**The Najdorf Variation**
(4b)	**The Boleslavsky Variation**
(5)	**The Kan structure**
(6)	**The Taimanov Variation**
(7)	**Offbeat Black systems**
(8)	**Closed Sicilian formations**

There are, of course, many more variations and branches of the Sicilian Defence, such as the c3 Sicilian (which falls into a category of its own) and the Pelikan variations, but these can only be covered briefly here.

Hans Kmoch, in *Pawn Power in Chess,* takes great pains to ensure that Louis Paulsen gets due credit for his contributions to a number of Sicilian Defence systems, including the Scheveningen, Boleslavsky, Paulsen and Dragon formations. Here we will place the Boleslavsky System, with Black's pawns on ...e5 and ...d6, in the same category as the Paulsen Variation, while systems with ...a6 and ...e6 (without an early ...d6) will be grouped under the Kan Variation.

1: The Scheveningen Structure

The Scheveningen pawn structure (where Black plays ...e6 and ...d6, typically with knights on f6 and c6) is characterized by solidity, flexibility, and compactness. The Sicilian and its diverse systems have a unique appeal in that *in general* they offer Black the superior pawn structure. This is quite a remarkable statement—let us see whether it is indeed true!

My first reason for drawing this conclusion is that in the Open Sicilian (after 3 d4 cxd4) Black emerges with two central pawns against White's lone e-pawn. Secondly, Black has a compact and sound structure, offering him excellent chances of gaining a lever with ...d5 after which he can exchange off White's only central pawn (the e4-pawn) or create a protected passed pawn if White's e-pawn advances to e5. It should also be mentioned that in the Sicilian Black emerges with more span (six squares, from c8 to c3 on his half-open c-file) than White has on his half-open d-file (five squares from d1 to d6). Sometimes White combats Black's span on the c-file with c3, but, in general, this doesn't do much for the mobility of White's queenside since b3 would then leave the White c-pawn backward.

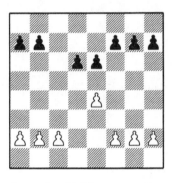

Inherently, Sicilian pawn formations do not offer White chances for improving the strength of his pawn structure. Let's see if this is true in the context of the Scheveningen formation. White's e-pawn is vulnerable and needs defence. If White creates a duo with f4, then both his e- and f-pawns need to be defended. If either of these pawns advances, to e5 or f5 respectively, then again White has little prospect of any improvement in his pawn structure —which may not alter much until the endgame. In other words White's primary chances in Sicilian structures lie in the middlegame, through kingside attack, while Black is considered to have excellent prospects in most of the ensuing endings.

In the Sicilian Scheveningen, when Black plays ...a6 and ...b5, this often has a multi-purpose, chain-reaction type of effect.

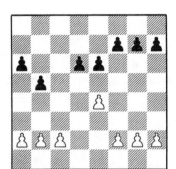

The purpose of ...a6 is to prevent a white knight from moving to b5 from where it can attack the slightly backward d-pawn. The move ...a6 also enables Black to follow with ...b5. When Black manages to play ...b5 his queenside attack gets going. The pawn on b5 usually threatens to attack a knight on c3 which defends the pawn on e4. So, in effect, the pawn on b5 has a direct influence on the centre.

Black's queenside expansion with ...b5 has the more general purpose of gaining space on the wing and creating a minority attack in which White's 3-2 majority on the queenside is not only nullified, but transformed into an isolated, possibly backward pawn.

In this *basic Sicilian* structure White's queenside majority is hampered by Black's minority advance and his c-pawn is somewhat backward.

Black's minority attack on the queenside can assume many forms, but its success usually depends on the presence of sufficient forces in order that enemy weaknesses may be attacked and exploited.

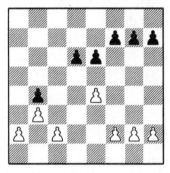

In this structure, White suffers from a very backward a-pawn (as in the Matulović-Fischer game shown earlier).

When Black's Scheveningen strategy is totally successful, it will look like a grand conception. For example a black knight might land on c4, via c6 and a5, or via d7 and b6, and be supported by a pawn which advances safely to d5, making everything look like a perfect picture for Black.

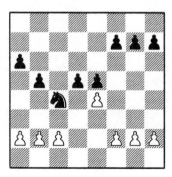

Sometimes Black needs to play ...e5 first (reaching the Boleslavsky structure) to ram White's e-pawn and then follow with the super-sound duo after ...d5.

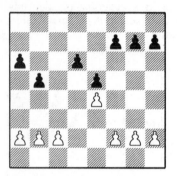

Black is always striving to achieve the lever ...d5. Sometimes, before playing ...e5, Black will play ...g6 in order to prevent a white knight on d4 moving to f5.

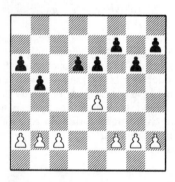

Of course this manoeuvre only works if the dark squares on Black's kingside can be adequately defended and if Black can follow with ...e5 and ...d5. Otherwise the move ...g6, combined with a backward d-pawn, will prove quite weakening for Black.

So what can go wrong for Black in Scheveningen Sicilian structures? Well, for example, the resulting diagrammed (Boleslavsky or Najdorf) structure can be very bad for Black if he is unable to contest the d5 square satisfactorily.

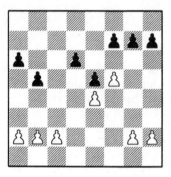

This is a very bad structure for Black (especially when he has a dark-squared bishop on e7 against a white knight on d5) and should be avoided under all circumstances where White has a "good" knight against a "bad" bishop.

At other times, when c3 has been played, the lever a4 may prove quite useful for White. In such cases the Black b-pawn can become a weakness, or if Black is compelled to capture on a4, then it is his a-pawn which might turn out to be weak.

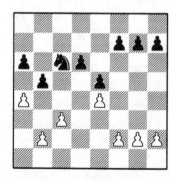

Let us now explore some typical Sicilian Scheveningen examples from actual play. The following game is taken from IM Craig Pritchett's wonderful treatise on the Sicilian Scheveningen. It illustrates how quickly Black's queenside play can be converted to a deadly kingside assault. It is a very common method in the Sicilian and one which I have come to call the "queenside-kingside swipe". In the examples which follow, it is remarkable just how flexible Black's Scheveningen formation is.

SCHEVENINGEN MASTERY LESSON 1

The Typical Scheveningen

■ Black executes the "queenside-kingside swipe".

■ White must attack (♕e1 – ♕g3)

■ The defence ...♔h8 is provocative

■ Black's queenside counterplay can take many forms (here, ...b4, axb4, ♘xb4)

■ White's commitment to a kingside attack means much may be left hanging on the queenside and/or centre

■ Black bishops to c6 and/or f6 can be very powerful in a kingside attack

---

Embedded in the following example is one main game, Wostyn-Sax, one main branch game with 10 a4

(instead of 10 ♕e1 as played in the Game 24, Karpov-Kasparov World Championship match, Moscow 1985), and two smaller branch continuations played in Anand-Kasparov, World Championship match, New York 1995.

Scheveningen (Game 1)
Wostyn-Sax
Nice Olympiad 1974

1 e4 c5 2 ♘f3 d6 3 d4 cxd4 4 ♘xd4 ♘f6 5 ♘c3 e6 6 ♗e2 a6
A very typical move order to reach this basic Scheveningen position, but over the first ten moves or so there are many transpositional possibilities.
7 0-0 ♕c7 8 f4 ♗e7 9 ♔h1 0-0

Wostyn-Sax:
Basic Branch Position
after 9...0-0

Now we will consider two major branches
10 ♕e1
Or 10 ♗e3, reaching the same game position. White is already making preparations for a kingside attack. Also 10 a4, the idea of which is to restrain Black's queenside expansion and subsequent counterplay.

10...♘c6 11 ♗e3

Here Kasparov could almost claim a patent on 11...♖e8, preparing counterplay on the e-file after the break ...e5. In the 1984-85 Kasparov-Karpov world title matches, play continued 12 ♗f3.

In Anand-Kasparov: Game 1, New York 1995 (fully annotated later), play went 12 ♕d2 ♗d7 13 ♖ad1 ♖ad8 14 ♘b3 ♗c8 (notice how Kasparov often uses this redeployment to prepare ...b6 and ...♗b7) 15 ♗f3 b6 16 ♕f2 ♘d7 17 ♘d4 ♗b7 and Black equalized without difficulty.

Games 3 and 5 of Anand-Kasparov, New York 1995, continued 12 ♗d3 ♘b4 13 a5 ♗d7 14 ♘f3 with very interesting play.

Our main game, **Wostyn-Sax** continued:

11...♗d7

Now we have the typical compact Scheveningen structure which I am very fond of. Black's bishops are, for the present, modestly placed, but in the middlegame they frequently become the most effective pieces on the board.

12 ♕g3 ♚h8

This is my favourite signature move in this position. Abayasakera-Kopec, Perth Open 1977, continued 13 ♗d3 ♖ac8 14 ♘xc6 ♗xc6 15 e5 dxe5 16 fxe5 ♘h5 17 ♕h3 g6 18 ♖ae1 ♖cd8 19 ♗h6 ♘g7 (If 20 ♘e4 ♗xe4 21 ♗xe4 ♕xe5) 20 ♖e2 ♖d4 21 ♕e3 ♖h4 22 ♗g5 ♖h5 23 ♗f4 ♗c5 24 ♕g3 ♘f5 25 ♕e1 ♗d4 26 ♘d1 ♘h4 27 ♗e4 ♗xe4 28 ♖xe4 ♕xc2 29 ♗d2 ♕d3 30 ♖xh4 ♖xh4 31 ♗b4 ♖e4 32 ♗xf8 ♖xe1 33 ♖xe1 ♕d2 34 ♖f1 ♕e2 0-1

The black king simply tries to sidestep any latent threats. Alternatives are 12...♘xd4 and 12...b5, both aiming to follow a trade on d4 with ...♗c6, gaining counterplay on White's e-pawn and on the queenside.

13 ♖ae1 b5

Black finally gets his counterplay going on the queenside.

14 a3 b4

Black could also play ...♖ab8 with similar threats.

15 axb4

After 15 ♘xc6 ♗xc6 16 axb4 ♘xe4 Black is better.

15...♘xb4 16 e5

White has to do something, otherwise he will be quickly overrun.

16...♘fd5 17 ♘xd5 ♘xd5 18 ♗f2?!

Pritchett blames this move for White's future problems. Instead he recommends ♗g1 or ♗c1.

18...♖ab8 19 ♗xa6?

This move loses but on 19 b3 dxe5 20 fxe5 ♗b4 Black still has queenside play.

19... ♖xb2 20 c4?

The cautious ♗d3 was better.

20...♘b4 21 ♕a3

White must have been relying on this move, but a very sharp combination dashes his hopes.

21...♖xf2! 22 ♖xf2 dxe5 23 fxe5 ♕a7!

Suddenly nearly all of White's pieces are hanging.

24 ♖b2 ♕xd4 25 ♖xb4 ♕d2 26 ♖eb1 ♗c6

The bishop finds its key square and immediately becomes a lethal weapon.

27 ♕c1

On 27 ♖4b2 ♗xg2+ 28 ♔g1 ♕d4+ wins.

27...♕xg2+ mate

Notice how Black has successfully completed the "queenside-kingside" swipe—where an initiative on the queenside is first converted to central control and then culminates in a kingside attack.

SCHEVENINGEN MASTERY LESSON 2

The Kasparov Scheveningen

■ Black employs the "queenside - kingside swipe"

■ Black uses the "Kasparov Manoeuvre" (...♕c7, ...♖e8, ...♗d7, ...♖ab8; then ...♗c8, ...b6 and ...♗b7)

■ After ...a6, ...b6 Black may play ...♘a5 with impunity since ♘xa5 bxa5 is often good for Black

■ The d7 square must be left open for the black knight on f6

■ Black uses the prophylactic defence ...♘d7 in anticipation of a White attack

■ Black redeploys the king's bishop with ...♗f8, ...g6, ...♗g7

■ White attacks with the rook lift to h3

■ When lines open up, Black's bishops on the long diagonal prove decisive

---

Scheveningen (Game 2)
A.Karpov-G.Kasparov
World Championship,
Moscow 1985

This proved to be the decisive and final game of the second World Championship match between Anatoly Karpov and his challenger, Garry Kasparov. The first match had been stopped by FIDE, headed by Florencio Campomanes, after 48 games, with Karpov leading 5-3 and 40 draws! Six wins were required for victory but Karpov was unable to achieve this despite having taken a 5-0 lead. In fact his health was failing as was his score in the match. To this day nobody is sure who benefited most from the curtailment of the match.

1 e4 c5 2 ♘f3 d6 3 d4 cxd4 4 ♘xd4 ♘f6 5 ♘c3 a6 6 ♗e2 e6 7 0-0 ♗e7 8 f4 0-0 9 ♔h1 ♕c7 10 a4 ♘c6 11 ♗e3 ♖e8 12 ♗f3 ♖b8 13 ♕d2 ♗d7 14 ♘b3 b6

Another typical Scheveningen middlegame. In the key 24th and final game of the 1985 match, play continued:

15 g4 ♗c8 16 g5 ♘d7 17 ♕f2

This avoids Sokolov-Ribli which continued favourably for Black after 17 ♗g2 ♘a5 (White dare not capture with ♘xa5 because Black gets too much play on the half-open b- and c-files) 18 ♕f2 ♘c4 19 ♗c1 and, thanks to his knight on c4, Black has an excellent position.

17...♗f8

Now White can meet 17...♘a5 with 18 ♖ad1 when 18...♘c4 19 ♗c1 is not so effective for Black.

18 ♗g2 ♗b7 19 ♖ad1 g6 20 ♗c1 ♖bc8?!

An alternative is ...♘c5 but in any case White is planning to lift a rook to the d- or e-file.

21 ♖d3 ♘b4 22 ♖h3 ♗g7 23 ♗e3

Many commentators suggested instead 23 f5 for White. Kasparov's position has turned out to be cramped but defensible with Karpov finding himself in the uncomfortable position of having to attack!

23...♖e7

Kasparov prepares for a wily defence of his second rank.

24 ♔g1 ♖ce8 25 ♖d1 f5 26 gxf6 ♘xf6 27 ♖g3 ♖f7

Now Kasparov coolly sheds a pawn while preparing for counterplay on the f4 square.

28 ♗xb6 ♕b8 29 ♗e3 ♘h5 30 ♖g4 ♘f6 31 ♖h4 g5

This starts the fireworks and had to be very carefully calculated.

32 fxg5 ♘g4

The queen sacrifice 33 ♕xf7+ (or 33 ♖xg4 ♖xf2 34 ♗xf2 ♘xc2) ♔xf7 34 ♖xg4 ♘xc2 would not be sufficient for White. Notice how the black bishops have come to life.

33 ♕d2 ♘xe3 34 ♕xe3 ♘xc2 35 ♕b6 ♗a8 36 ♖xd6

The ending after 36 ♕xb8? would clearly favour Black.

36...♖b7 37 ♕xa6 ♖xb3

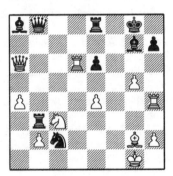

Play is boardwide but Black is a piece ahead and all his forces are active.

38 ♖xe6 ♖xb2 39 ♕c4 ♔h8 40 e5 ♕a7+ 41 ♔h1 ♗xg2+ 42 ♔xg2 ♘d4+

An excellent demonstration of the explosive power of the Scheveningen Variation, tailor made for the tense match situation!

43 ♔f1 0-1

SCHEVENINGEN MASTERY LESSON 3

More "Kasparov Manoeuvres"

■ Black uses the "Kasparov Manoeuvre" (...♕c7, ...♖e8, ...♗d7, ...♖ab8; then ...♗c8, ...b6 and ...♗b7)

■ After ...a6, ...b6 Black may play ...♘a5 with impunity since ♘xa5 bxa5 is often good for Black

■ The d7 square must be left open for the black knight on f6

■ Black uses the prophylactic defence ...♘d7 in anticipation of a White attack

■ Black uses the liquidation manoeuvre ...♘xd4 to slow White's attack

■ The lever ...e5 with the trade fxe5 ♗xe5 serves Black well

■ Black attains full equality after ...♗c6

Scheveningen (Game 3) ♟
V.Anand-G.Kasparov
World Championship,
New York 1995

As Black, Garry Kasparov contested no less than five games with the Scheveningen against his challenger, Vishy Anand. Although he did not win any of them, he provided a pretty good model of how to handle the Black side in this opening.

1 e4 c5 2 ♘f3 d6 3 d4 cxd4 4 ♘xd4 ♘f6 5 ♘c3 a6 6 ♗e2 e6 7 a4

Anand goes for restraint, preventing Black from playing ...b5.

7...♘c6 8 0-0 ♗e7 9 ♗e3 0-0 10 f4 ♕c7

Typical of Kasparov's favourite setup and aimed at preventing e5 by White, while preparing it for Black.

11 ♔h1 ♖e8 12 ♕d2

12 ♕e1 has been played, but White has no particular advantage after 12...♘xd4 13 ♗xd4 e5 14 fxe5 dxe5 15 ♕g3 ♗d8 etc, which follows an earlier game of Kasparov's. Also possible is 12 ♘b3 b6 13 ♕e1 ♖b8 etc.

12...♗d7 13 ♖ad1

On 13 ♗f3 ♖ab8 14 ♕f2 e5 15 ♘f5 ♗xf5 16 exf5 ♕a5 17 g4 (as in King-Mainka, Dortmund 1987). After, for example, 17...e4 18 ♗e2 d5 19 ♗b6 ♕b4 20 g5 e3 21 ♗xe3 d4 22 gxf6 dxe3 23 ♕g2 ♗xf6 Black has good play.

13...♖ad8

13...♘xd4 14 ♕xd4 e5 15 ♕d3 ♖ad8 16 ♕c4 was played in Sznapik-Wojtkiewicz, match, Poland 1991. On 16 ♗f3 b5 17 axb5 axb5 18 ♘d5 ♘xd5 19 exd5 exf4 Black had a sound and compact

position, Sznapik-Ftačnik, Haifa 1989.

14 ♘b3

Another continuation is 14 ♗f3 ♘a5 15 ♕e1 ♘c4 16 ♗c1 e5 17 ♘de2 b5 as in Wolff-De Boer, Wijk aan Zee Open, 1993, which is fully playable for Black.

14...♗c8 15 ♗f3 b6 16 ♕f2 ♘d7

17 ♘d4

After 17 g4 Black replies 17...♗f6 with the idea of ...♗xc3. And on 17 e5 dxe5 18 ♖xd7 (if 18 ♗xc6 ♕xc6 19 fxe5 f5 20 ♘d4 ♕c4) 18...♗xd7 19 ♗xb6 ♕b8 20 ♗xd8 ♖xd8 21 ♗xc6 ♗xc6 22 fxe5 ♖f8 Black's two bishops offer excellent compensation.

17...♗b7 18 ♗h5 ♖f8 19 ♕g3 ♘xd4 20 ♗xd4 ♗f6 21 ♗e2 e5 22 fxe5 ♗xe5 23 ♕f2 ♘c5

24 ♗f3

Criticized in the post mortem by Kasparov who preferred 24 ♗xe5 dxe5 25 ♖xd8 ♖xd8 (25...♕xd8 26 a5) 26 ♗c4 ♘xe4 27 ♕xf7+ ♕xf7 28 ♖xf7 ♖d4 (28...♔h8 29 ♖xb7 ♘xc3 30 h3 ♘xa4 31 b3 b5=) 29 ♗a2 (29 ♗b3 ♘xc3 30 ♖xb7+ ♔f8 31 h3 ♘xa4 32 ♖f7+ ♔e8 33 ♖xg7±) 29...♘xc3 30 bxc3 ♗d5! (but not 30...♖xa4? 31 ♗b3).

24...♖fe8

With excellent minor pieces on c5 and e5, Black is very happy with his compact pawn structure.

25 h3 a5 26 ♖fe1 ♗c6 27 b3

27...h6

Black has two other moves leading to approximate equality. The first is 27...♕b7 28 ♘d5 ♗xd4 29 ♖xd4 ♖e5 30 ♖ed1 ♖de8 31 ♘c3 when Black has two alternatives: (a) 31...f5 32 exf5 (a1) 32...♖xf5 33 ♗xc6 ♖xf2 34 ♗xb7 ♘xb7 (34...♖xc2 35 ♗d5+) 35 ♖4d2=; (a2) 32...♗xf3 33 ♕xf3 ♕xf3 34 gxf3; (b) 31...♘xe4 32 ♘xe4 ♗xe4 33 ♗xe4 ♖xe4 34 ♖xe4 ♕xe4 35 ♖xd6=; The second alternative is 27...♕e7 28 ♖e2 ♕g5 29 ♗xe5 dxe5 30 ♖ed2 with equality.

½-½

SCHEVENINGEN MASTERY LESSON 4

Solid with Counterplay

■ Black develops solidly with ...♘f6, ...♗e7, ...♘c6, and ...♗d7

■ The d7 square must be left open for the black knight on f6 with ...♗e8

■ Black uses the prophylactic defence ...♘d7 in anticipation of a White attack

■ Black equalizes with ...♘c5

Scheveningen (Game 4) ♦
J.Fichtl-B.Malich
Halle 1974

A more constrained approach by White against the Scheveningen is the attempt to restrict Black's queenside play by 10 ♘b3 followed by a4. The following game fragment illustrates typical positions reached from this kind of continuation.

1 e4 c5 2 ♘f3 e6 3 d4 cxd4 4 ♘xd4 ♘f6 5 ♘c3 d6 6 ♗e2 ♗e7 7 0-0 0-0 8 f4 ♘c6

The important thing to remember in nearly all variations of the Sicilian Defence is that Black must always be prepared to respond to White's attacking advances f5 or e5.

9 ♗e3 ♗d7 10 ♘b3

This move is primarily aimed at avoiding exchanges which generally favour Black's strategic goals in the Sicilian.

10...a6 11 a4

And now White prevents Black's queenside expansion. Here Black has a number of moves, including ...♘a5?!, ...♕c7, ...♘b4!?, and ...♖c8 but the soundest continuation is...

11...b6

Protecting the dark squares on the queenside.

12 ♗f3 ♕c7 13 ♕e2 ♖fc8

Fichtl-Malich, Halle, 1974 continued:

14 g4 ♗e8 15 ♖ad1 !?

More logical is 15 g5 ♘d7 16 ♗g2.

15...♘d7 16 g5 ♘c5

Black has dynamic equality.

> **SCHEVENINGEN MASTERY LESSON 5**
>
> **Counterplay using the e5 square**
>
> ■ Black develops solidly with ...♘f6, ...♗e7, ...♘c6, and ...♗d7
>
> ■ Black uses the ...♘b4 manoeuvre coupled with ...e5 to obtain counterplay
>
> ■ Black gains good play from the e5 square for his knight after the exchange ...exf4

Scheveningen (Game 5)
R.McKay-D.Kopec
Scottish Championship,
St. Andrews 1981

1 e4 e6 2 d4 c5 3 ♘f3 cxd4 4 ♘xd4 ♘f6 5 ♘c3 d6 6 ♗e2 ♗e7 7 0-0 ♘c6 8 ♔h1 0-0 9 f4 ♗d7 10 ♘b3

This move is rather passive and the source of White's later troubles.

10...a6 11 a4 ♖c8 12 ♗e3 ♘b4 13 ♗d3 e5!

This "ram" prevents White from playing e5 and foreshadows ...d5 as a possible lever for Black. It also puts the question to White's e4/f4 duo.

14 a5 ♗e6!

Black's moves are easy to play, involving as they do a concentration of forces on the centre and an eye for simplification.

15 ♘d2 exf4 16 ♗b6

If 16 ♗xf4 ♘g4.

16...♕e8 17 ♖xf4 ♘d7 18 ♗d4 ♘e5

On this square, Black's knight will turn out to be very comfortable —and very annoying for White!

19 ♗e2 ♗d8 20 ♖f1 ♘ec6 21 ♗b6 ♗xb6 22 axb6 ♘d4

The game now turns decidedly in Black's favour as it is clear that the white pawn on b6 is overextended and White has no particular play. White should try ♗d3 and accept the reality of his situation.

23 ♘f3 ♘dxc2

Now Black wins the exchange and White has no compensation. Hence the game is essentially over.

24 ♖c1 ♘e3 25 ♕xd6 ♘xf1 26 ♕xb4 ♘e3 27 ♕d4 ♘c4 28 e5 ♕d8 29 ♕e4 ♘d2 30 ♕xb7 ♘xf3 31 ♗xf3 ♖b8 32 ♕xa6 ♕xb6 33 ♕xb6 ♖xb6 34 ♘a4 ♖b4 35 ♘c5 ♖xb2 36 ♘xe6 fxe6 37 h3 ♖b5 38 ♖e1 ♖f5 39 ♗g4 ♖bxe5 40 ♖a1 ♖f6 41 ♖a8+ ♔f7 42 ♔h2 ♔g6 43 ♖a6 ♖e1 44 ♗f3 ♖f5 45 ♔g3 ♔f6 46 ♔f2 ♖c1 47 ♔g3 ♖c3 48 ♖a4 g5 49 h4 h6 50 hxg5+ hxg5 51 ♖a6 ♖f4 52 ♖b6 ♔f5 53 ♖b8 e5 54 ♖f8+ ♔g6 55 ♖g8+ ♔f6 56 ♖f8+ ♔g7 57 ♖xf4 gxf4+ 0-1

Scheveningen (Game 6)
W. Browne-D. Kopec
25 Board Simultaneous,
New York 1970

In August 1970, 21 year old Walter Browne was brimming with success, having just been officially awarded the Grandmaster title. I was 16 at the time and a rising expert. After a big Open tournament in

New York, Browne gave a 25 board simultaneous exhibition in which I took part and was one of the few lucky winners. I present this game, not just because I won, but because it is an excellent example of all the good things the Sicilian Scheveningen structure can bring.

1 e4 c5 2 ♘f3 d6 3 ♘c3 ♘c6 4 d4 cxd4 5 ♘xd4 e6 6 f4 ♗d7 7 ♗e3 ♘f6 8 ♕f3 ♗e7

I remember fearing 0-0-0 here but then Black would still continue with ...a6 followed by ...♘xd4 and ...♗c6, with other possibilities such as ...♖c8. White usually reacts with an attack by g4-g5, but for some reason, on this board, Browne was in a mellow mood.

9 ♗d3

I was happy to see this move which gave me the chance to complete my Sicilian setup before the action started.

9...a6 10 0-0 ♕c7 11 f5?!

This move also came as surprise since it compromises White's pawn structure and concedes the e5 square.

11...♘e5 12 ♕h3 ♘eg4 13 fxe6 fxe6

Black now has an enviably compact centre and White must relinquish his dark-squared bishop.

14 ♖ae1 ♘xe3 15 ♕xe3

This recapture is necessary in the light of possibilities such as ...♕b6 or ...f5.

15...♕c5!

This move comes just in time since 16 e5 can be met by ...♘g4. Black is now edging towards an ending.

16 ♘b3 ♕xe3+ 17 ♖xe3

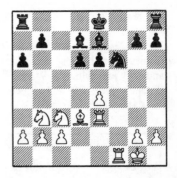

Browne probably thought he would easily outplay me in this ending. I probably expected him to outplay me too, but Black's structure is so solid and strong that this is just not possible. Yes, Black is lagging in development, but he has two bishops and control of the key central squares with no weaknesses. This is precisely what I mean when I state that endings from the Sicilian often tend to favour Black. Notice that White already has three pawn islands, including an isolated e-pawn, while Black's three pairs of pawns are very compact and safe. It is noteworthy that White already suffers from the absence of his dark-squared bishop.

17...b5

So I start my queenside counterplay, even with an incomplete development, but that is because White can't hurt me. Note that 18 e5? is met by ...♘g4.

18 a3 ♗d8!

A very pleasing redeployment which gave me a good idea where the black king should reside. Here 19 ♖g3 looks like an improvement but after ...0-0 Black would have few problems. What a wonderful ending the Sicilian can give

Black—and he doesn't even have to earn it!

19 ♔h1 ♗b6 20 ♖ef3 ♔e7 21 h3 ♖af8

Black's game is very comfortable.

22 ♔h2 ♗c6 23 ♖e1 h5

It is interesting for me, today, to see how each relatively passive move by Browne gave me more confidence to play aggressively. Now ...♘g4+ is threatened.

24 ♔h1 h4 25 ♔h2 e5 26 ♖ef1 g5 27 ♔h1 ♘h5 28 ♖xf8 ♘g3+ 29 ♔h2 ♖xf8 30 ♖xf8 ♔xf8 31 ♘d2 ♔f7 32 ♘f1 ♘xf1+ 33 ♗xf1 ♗d4 34 ♗d3 ♗xc3 35 bxc3

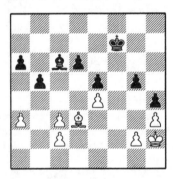

The transformation in pawn structure proves sufficient for Black to achieve victory. He has three critical advantages: (1) better bishop, (2) better pawns, and (3) better king.

35...d5 36 exd5 ♗xd5 37 ♔g1 e4 38 ♗e2 e3 39 ♔f1 ♔f6 40 ♗g4 ♔e5 41 ♗c8 ♗c4+ 42 ♔e1 a5 43 ♗a6 ♔d6 44 a4 ♔c5 45 axb5 a4 White Resigns

I lost closely in the only tournament game Browne and I have played, at the 1976 Canadian Open. We've been good friends since, but I'm still looking for an opportunity to get my revenge.

SCHEVENINGEN MASTERY LESSON 7

Trading on d4 and Regrouping via d7 with Lever Action

■ Black uses the liquidation manoeuvre ...♘xd4 to slow White's attack

■ The d7 square must be left open for Black's knight on f6

■ Black regroups with ...♘d7 in anticipation of a White attack

■ Black gets queenside play against the white king with ...b5, ...b4 and ...♘e5, ...♘c4 etc

■ Black plays a timely ...e5 and ...d5 for central counterplay

Scheveningen (Game 7)
V.Topalov-G.Kasparov
Amsterdam, 1995

Over the past few years a system of play for White known as the "English Attack" has become popular. So-called because it is favoured by English Grandmasters such as Short, Nunn, and Adams, it is based on the move f3 in connection with queenside castling and a pawn storm. Let us see how Kasparov deals with this problem.

1 e4 c5 2 ♘f3 ♘c6 3 d4 cxd4 4 ♘xd4 e6 5 ♘c3 d6 6 ♗e3 ♘f6 7 f3

The English Attack.

7...♗e7 8 g4

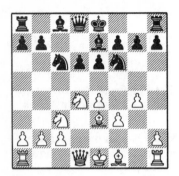

It is always instructive to see how Kasparov handles a direct assault.

8...0-0 9 ♕d2 a6 10 0-0-0 ♘xd4 11 ♗xd4 b5 12 ♔b1

After 12 g5 ♘d7 13 f4 b4 14 ♘e2 ♗b7 followed by ...e5 gives Black a nice game.

12...♗b7 13 h4 ♖c8 14 g5 ♘d7

This knight move is important both for defence and also counterattack in the centre and queenside.

15 ♖g1 b4 16 ♘e2 ♘e5!

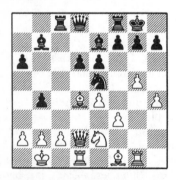

A strong move (and a typical one) in that it achieves all of Black's strategic goals with tempo. Of course now 17 ♗xe5 dxe5 favours Black because of his two bishops and central control.

17 ♖g3 ♘c4 18 ♕c1 e5

Kasparov starts to take over the initiative.

19 ♗f2 a5 20 ♗g2

Only now does White complete his development. This move looks ugly but it prepares f4.

20...♗a6 21 ♖e1 a4 22 ♗h3 ♖c6

Kasparov is taking over every part of the board except for the lower right quadrant.

23 ♕d1

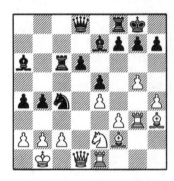

23...d5!

Black's key lever often comes when least expected! Now 24 ♕xd5 is impossible because of 24...♖d6! trapping the white queen.

24 exd5 ♖d6 25 f4 ♖xd5 26 ♖d3

26...♘a3+

Not surprisingly, Kasparov now finds a winning combination.

27 bxa3 ♗xd3 28 cxd3 ♖xd3 White Resigns.

SCHEVENINGEN MASTERY LESSON 8
Counterplay against the Keres Attack

■ Black plays ...h6 against the Keres Attack

■ The d7 square must be left open for the black knight on f6

■ Black regroups with ...♘d7 in anticipation of a White attack

■ Black delays castling

■ Black gets queenside play against the white king with ...b5, ...b4 and ...♘c5, ...a5 etc

■ Black successfully opens lines to the white king with ...a4, ...axb3, etc

Scheveningen (Game 8)
A.Ivanov-D.Kopec
Stratton Mountain Open, USA 1994

A very popular line against the Scheveningen is the Keres Attack (6 g4). This system aims to gain space on the kingside and discourage Black from castling there. Yet White's pawn advances on the kingside cost time and may also be weakening. The following gamelet was certainly a satisfying draw from my point of view because I was only too aware that my opponent knew a lot more about this opening than I did, and had much more experience with it. Again I do not attribute the result to anything more than the innate soundness of the Sicilian Scheveningen.

1 e4 c5 2 ♘f3 e6 3 d4 cxd4 4 ♘xd4 ♘f6 5 ♘c3 d6 6 g4 h6 7 ♗g2 ♗e7

Black can also play 7...♘c6.

8 h4 ♘fd7 9 g5 hxg5 10 hxg5 ♖xh1+ 11 ♗xh1 g6

Not 11...♗xg5? 12 ♘xe6 winning quickly. White's g6 lever must be stopped—hence the text move.

12 f4 ♘c6 13 ♘f3 a6 14 b3

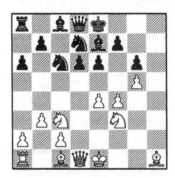

14...♕c7

Since White is pretty much committed to fianchettoing his queen's bishop, perhaps simply 14...♕a5 is indicated. Then after 15 ♗b2 ♗f8 is possible. Notice that Black has achieved a comfortable opening without castling. In some Sicilian variations it is important for Black to delay castling, if only to keep White guessing where his king will eventually land up.

15 ♗b2 b5 16 ♕d2 ♗b7?!

16...♘c5 was more accurate since ...b4 would then be threatened.

17 0-0-0 ♘c5 18 ♕e3 ♖c8 19 ♘e1 b4 20 ♘e2 a5 21 ♔b1 a4 22 ♘c1 axb3 ½-½

A draw was agreed because White was drifting into time trouble. After 23 axb3 Black would continue with 23...♘a7, heading for b5 and then c3 or a3.

**SCHEVENINGEN MASTERY
LESSON 9**

**Restraining, Trapping and
Countering**

■ **Black halts White's kingside
play with ...♘h7 and ...g5**

■ **Black gets queenside play
with ...b4 and ...♖b8**

■ **Black plays to trap the ♘a4
with ...♗d7**

■ **White misses an important
opportunity with 22 ♗g4**

■ **Black gets tremendous
counterplay with ...b3**

Scheveningen (Game 9)
J.Stewart-D.Kopec
Correspondence Game,
4th North Atlantic
Team Tournament 1995-1997

Correspondence play is an excellent medium to test one's ideas and systems. Games often take one to two years and give a player the opportunity to learn complex opening systems. This game was played in the 4th North Atlantic Team Tournament (1995-1997), USA vs. Scotland, where I played board two for the USA and scored a Correspondence IM norm with +3, -1, =6.

1 e4 c5 2 ♘f3 d6 3 d4 cxd4 4 ♘xd4 ♘f6 5 ♘c3 e6 6 g4 h6
This is a standard continuation against the Keres Attack. The other

main alternatives are 6...a6 and 6...♘c6. With ...h6 Black tries to slow down a little White's kingside assault.

7 h4 ♘c6 8 ♖g1 h5

The standard move in this position against the Keres Attack (6 g4). I checked Craig Pritchett's book *The Sicilian Scheveningen* (Batsford, 1977) in preparation for this continuation. It is important that Black can meet 9 g5 with 9...♘g4 when 10 f3 ♘e5 is fine as White has rather overextended himself. On the other hand, 9...♘d7 would be an error because it invites the effective 10 g6—a main theme to beware of: White plays g4 precisely to play g5 and g6. Nevertheless, even after 9...♘d7 10 g6!?, Black still has some resources because the white pawn on h4 is hanging.

An earlier over-the-board game of mine against Ed Formanek, Phillips & Drew, London, 1982, reached this same position and continued 9 g5 ♘g4 10 ♘b3 ♕b6 11 ♕e2 g6 12 ♖g3 a6 13 f3 ♘ge5 14 f4 ♘g4 15 ♗h3 ♗g7 16 ♗d2 ♗d7 17 0-0-0 ♕f2 18 ♖g2 ♕xe2 19 ♘xe2 e5 20 ♘c3 ♗e6 21 ♘d5 0-0-0 22 ♗c3

&b8 23 ♖e2 ♖he8 24 ♖f1 ♗h8 25
fxe5 ♘cxe5 26 ♘d4 ♗xd5 27 exd5
♘c4 28 ♖fe1 ♖xe2 29 ♘xe2 ♗e5
when Black had full equality.

9 gxh5 ♘xh5 10 ♗g5

10...♘f6

This was a new move introduced
by Ulf Andersson in the 1970s.
Before, Black used to play 10...♕c7
with some discomfort. Karpov-
Kasparov, World Championship
match, Moscow 1984, continued 11
♕d2 ♕b6 12 ♘b3 ♗d7 13 0-0-0 a6,
ending in a draw in 36 moves.

11 ♗e2 ♕b6

My idea was to force the white
knight on d4 to make a decision so I
could assess how to complete my
development.

12 ♘b3 a6

Now I anticipated ♗e3 and ♘b5
so played ...a6 in order to continue
with ...♕c7 and ...b5 etc.

13 h5

In Pritchett's book and indeed
subsequent games, this is seen as the
key move—to squeeze Black's
kingside development.

13...♕c7 14 h6 ♘h7!

Surprisingly, to me, this is almost
an "only move". Nevertheless it's
reasonable and helps to relieve
Black's problems.

15 ♗e3 g5

This move is important in Black's
scheme of finding counterplay. The
white pawn on h6 has been effectively blockaded and Black can look
forward to capturing it at a later moment, after completing his development. Here 16 ♗xg5? ♘xg5 17
♖xg5 ♗xh6 is not particularly appe-
tizing for White.

**16 ♕d2 b5 17 0-0-0 b4 18 ♘a4
♖b8**

And now we see that by quite
simple means Black is starting to
muster counterplay. Black threatens
...♗d7 and ...♘d8 winning material.
It is important to bear in mind that
this was a correspondence game so
White could not resort to unsound
tactics.

19 f4

White naturally tries to open lines against the black king.

19...gxf4 20 ♗xf4 e5

And Black reacts accordingly— switching in good time to the Boleslavsky structure. Note that White's knights do not have easy access to d5 and therefore cannot exploit the hole created on that square. Moreover Black is prepared to defend f7 with ...♘d8 if necessary.

21 ♗e3 ♗d7

It is hard to believe that White can really stand worse in this position because the black king is caught in the centre and his rook and knight are out of play on the kingside. So I fed this position to Fritz and it found 22 ♗g4! which is quite logical, exploiting as it does the weaknesses on Black's light squares by trading off the key defender (and the piece which threatens a4). What Fritz found was 22 ♗g4 ♗xg4 23 ♖xg4 ♘d8 24 ♕g2 ♕c6 25 ♖g8 ♖xg8 26 ♕xg8 ♕xe4 and White stands slightly better—no doubt due to Black's poor piece coordination. My main idea was to answer 22 ♗xa6 with 22...♘a5 leading to a very complex game and counterplay for Black. But 22...♘d8 may be

Black's best, leading at least to material equality.

22 ♘ac5 dxc5 23 ♘xc5 ♘f6

The black knight finally returns to play—just in time.

24 ♗g5 ♘d4

25 ♗xf6

Here Fritz finds White's best continuation: 25 ♘xa6 ♕c8 26 ♘xb8 ♘xe4 27 ♘xd7! ♘xd2? 28 ♘f6+ with advantage to White. But Black can play instead 27...♕xd7, with ...♘xg5, ...♗xh6 and complex play to follow. However, after 25...♕c8, I and Fritz also saw 26 ♗xf6 (26 ♘xb8 b3 27 ♔b1 bxc2+ 28 ♔a1 ♘xe4 decides) 26...♗xh6 wins.

25...♕xc5 26 ♗xh8

The only move but White is lost in any case.

26...b3 27 ♔b1 bxc2+ 28 ♔a1 ♖xb2 29 ♗c4 cxd1=♕+

After 30 ♕xd1 ♕xc4 31 ♔xb2 ♗a3+ 32 ♔xa3 ♕c3+ 33 ♕b3 ♘c2 is mate.

0-1

The following three examples all illustrate Scheveningens where White tries to combine central play with an early g4. As will be seen, this move must be dealt with energetically.

SCHEVENINGEN MASTERY LESSON 10

Vigorously meeting an early g4

■ When White plays an early f4 Black must always be ready for e5 or f5

■ Black gets queenside and central counterplay with ...b4

■ Black must respond vigorously to an early g4

■ The move ...e5 will break up White's trio on g4, f4 and e4

■ After ...e5, ♘f5, the white knight must be quickly eliminated

■ Black should have long-term chances against White's overextended and ruptured pawn structure

Scheveningen (Game 10)
J.Peters-D.Kopec
Lloyds Bank Masters, London 1978

1 e4 e6 2 d4 c5
The Franco-Sicilian move order to reach a Sicilian. Bent Larsen used to play this with great success, as Black, when games sometimes continued 3 d5 cxd5 4 exd5 d6 5 ♘c3 ♘f6 6 ♘f3 ♗e7 etc.

3 ♘f3
Now there is really little else Black can do than transpose into the Sicilian Defence.

3...cxd4 4 ♘xd4 ♘f6 5 ♘c3 d6 6 f4
When White plays an early f4 it is always important for Black to be ready for the possibility of e5 or f5 driving his king's knight away from a safe square and disrupting his smooth development.

6...a6 7 ♗e2 b5!?
This is quite double-edged. The more solid Scheveningen move is 7...♕c7, but then Black must be prepared for g4 in any case.

8 ♗f3 e5
Seemingly a forced move. This position has arisen because of Black's sharp and risky 7...b5!?.

9 ♘f5 ♕c7 10 g4

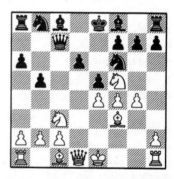

Black must react vigorously to this outright declaration of aggression. Interestingly, despite Black's abundance of pawn moves in the opening, his position is sound and he has good play.

10...b4 11 fxe5 dxe5 12 ♘d5 ♘xd5 13 exd5 ♗xf5
Black is quite prepared to play the exchange down after 14 d6 ♗xd6 15 ♗xa8 etc. The white king will have difficulty finding shelter. In any case, after 14 gxf5 ♗d6 with

...♘d7 to follow, Black's game would be very solid. In my opinion White is somewhat overextended which is the typical outcome of a very early g4!?. My draw offer was a psychological one. Peters was leading the tournament and from previous encounters he knew I was a dangerous opponent. He therefore decided that discretion was the better part of valour. ½-½

SCHEVENINGEN MASTERY LESSON 11

Black counters central neglect with ...♘c6

■ Sometimes ...♘c6 is a strong way for Black to counter an early g4

■ After ♘xc6 bxc6; g5 ♘d7 Black has a strong centre and a flexible position

■ Sometimes after ...gxf5 Black's doubled-isolated f-pawns can be strong - defending the king and supporting the outpost on the e4 square

---

Scheveningen (Game 11)
J.Drexel-D.Kopec
Correspondence, 1990

1 d4 e6
Black wants to play a French or Nimzo-Indian.
2 ♘f3 c5
However, by a rather unusual move order, the game transposes into a Sicilian Defence.

3 e4 cxd4 4 ♘xd4 ♘f6 5 ♘c3 d6
So now we arrive at a standard Scheveningen.
6 g3 a6 7 ♗g2 ♗e7
White's slightly passive setup, with the fianchetto of his king's bishop, allows Black more flexibility.
8 0-0 0-0 9 f4
A rather aggressive move which Black hopes to meet with a timely ...e5.
9...♕c7 10 g4?!

White makes it clear that he wants to push Black off the board. As Black has not made any obvious errors, this should not be possible.
10 ♘c6!
The proper response to White's blatant aggression. The point is that if now 11 g5? Black can reply with 11...♘xd4 12 gxf6 ♗xf6, or 12 ♕xd4 d5!, more than equalizing.
11 ♘xc6 bxc6
Black's centre is now very strong.
12 g5 ♘d7 13 f5 exf5
At least White has been consistent. There is no reason for Black to endure the complications of f6.
14 exf5
White's pawns on f5/g5 look dangerous but White has no centre left.
14...d5 15 ♔h1

Had White played 15 f6 then 15...♗c5+ 16 ♔h1 g6 was possible. Then on 17 ♗f4 ♗d6 18 ♗xd6 ♕xd6, White has yet to demonstrate that his kingside pawns are not overextended.

15...♗d6 16 ♕h5 g6 17 ♕h4

If 17 fxg6 hxg6 18 ♕h4 ♘e5 and it is only Black who can stand better.

White probably underestimated the strength of Black's last move.

17 gxf5

The unique theme of the *doubled isolated f-pawns* strikes. If now 18 ♖xf5 ♘e5 is very strong. Given that the f5-pawn cannot be captured, then Black's grip on e4 assures him of an advantage.

18 ♖f3 ♖e8 0-1

White resigns abruptly. Bearing in mind that this was a correspondence game, it is not so surprising. On 19 ♖h3 ♘f8 Black has many trumps up his sleeve, including ...♖b8-b4 and sole possession of the open e-file, not to mention a possible exchange sacrifice on e4. Understandably White does not see much pleasure in what is to follow and his resignation is a simple admission of this.

SCHEVENINGEN MASTERY LESSON 12

Black counters an early g4 with ...♘xd4 and ...e5

■ When White plays an early f4 Black must always be ready for e5 or f5

■ Black must respond vigorously to an early g4

■ The move ...♘c6 coupled with ...♘xd4 and ...e5 will break up White's trio on g4, f4 and e4

■ Black should have long-term chances against White's overextended and ruptured pawn structure

Scheveningen (Game 12)
L.Schneider-D.Kopec
Gausdal 1983

1 e4 e6 2 d4 c5

A move order which can be used to reach the Sicilian Defence unless White now decides to play 3 d5.

3 ♘f3 cxd4 4 ♘xd4 ♘f6 5 ♘c3 d6 6 f4 a6 7 ♕f3 ♕c7 8 g4

This is akin to the Browne game, shown earlier, except that here White chooses a very aggressive pawn thrust.

8...♘c6

A useful way to put the question to White.

9 ♗e3 ♘xd4 10 ♗xd4 e5

Black thereby destroys the white pawn trio.

11 fxe5 dxe5 12 ♕g3 ♗d6 13 ♗g1 ♗b4

The bishop has served its purpose on d6 and so Black jumps at the opportunity to wreck the white king's shelter on both sides of the board.

14 ♗g2 ♗xc3+ 15 bxc3 ♗xg4 16 ♗d4 0-0-0

Anxious to connect the rooks; an alternative was 16...♘d7.

17 ♗xe5 ♕c4 18 ♕e3

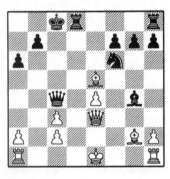

18...♖he8

Black certainly had some alternatives, including ...♘d7 or ...♘e8, e.g 18...♘d7 19 ♗xg7 ♖hg8 etc. Even 18...♘d5!? followed by ...♖he8 comes into consideration, e.g. after 19 exd5 ♖he8 White finds it hard to make a move.

19 ♗xf6 gxf6 20 ♖f1 ♖e5 21 ♖xf6

Black appears to have stood better throughout, but I could not find any forced win.

21...♖de8 22 ♖f4 ♗h5 23 ♔f2 ♖c5 24 ♗h3+ ♔b8 25 ♖f5 ♖xf5+ 26 ♗xf5 ♗g6 27 ♖e1 ♗xf5 28 ♕f4+ ♕c7 29 ♕xf5

White avoids the lost king and pawn ending after 29 ♕xc7+ ♔xc7 30 exf5 ♖xe1 and ...♔d6 etc.

29...♕xh2+ 30 ♔f3 ♖c8 31 ♖e3 ♕h1+ 32 ♔e2 ♕g2+ 33 ♕f2 ♕g4+ 34 ♔d2 ♕e6 35 ♕h2+ ♔a7 36 ♕xh7 ♕xa2 37 ♕f5 ♖d8+ 38 ♖d3 ♖xd3+ 39 ♔xd3 a5 40 c4 ♕a3+ 41 ♔e2 ½-½

2: The Dragon Structure

The Dragon Sicilian structure, offering a very rugged, compact and healthy group of five pawns, is one of the most solid setups Black can have.

The structure is very hard for White to break down, and Black can depend on excellent play from his g7-bishop which breathes fire along the a1-h8 diagonal.

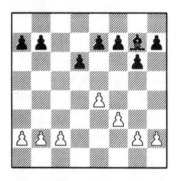

If White castles queenside against the Dragon, e.g., as in the Yugoslav Attack variation, then Black will endeavour to muster serious play on the queenside in the race to get to the opponent's king. Normally Black's attack will include some or all of the following motifs:

(1) Play on the half-open c-file with doubled rooks and possibly a queen bearing down on c2.

(2) A storm of pawns on the queenside, including the moves ...b5 and ...a5 followed by ...b4, ...a4, etc., trying to force open lines against the white king.

(3) An exchange sacrifice on c3 (...♖xc3 forcing bxc3) in order to destroy the pawn structure in front of the white king. Sometimes this motif, coupled with the capture of the white e-pawn on e4, can be very strong—even in the endgame.

(4) Occupation of c4 with a knight, via e5 or a5, resulting in tremendous pressure on b2.

Interestingly, these four possible themes, promoting queenside counterplay, are available to Black even if White castles kingside (without f2-f3) in the standard Dragon. In this case none of these attacking motifs may be as dangerous for White, since his king resides on the right wing, but nor does White get such strong attacking play on the kingside. Furthermore, Black's queenside minority attack can still be a problem for White.

The following early Dragon game illustrates its appeal to original attacking players.

A.Suetin-L.Szabo
Leningrad 1967

1 e4 c5 2 ♘f3 g6 3 d4 ♗g7 4 ♘c3 cxd4 5 ♘xd4 ♘c6 6 ♗e3 ♘f6 7 ♗c4 d6 8 f3 ♗d7 9 ♕d2 ♖c8 10 ♗b3 ♘e5 11 h4 ♘c4 12 ♗xc4 ♖xc4 13 0-0-0 h5 14 ♔b1 0-0 15 ♘de2 b5 16 ♗h6

For players who like to attack, are prepared to take chances, have strong nerves and relish the possibility of delivering blood-curdling attacks (as well as enduring them), the Black side of the Yugoslav Attack Dragon can be the perfect potion.

Theory has advanced considerably since this game, but, in a sense, not *that* much! Anand-Kasparov (World Championship match 1995) followed exactly this opening sequence up to 16...♕a5.

16...♕a5 17 ♗g5 b4 18 ♘d5 ♘xd5 19 ♕xd5 ♖c5 20 ♕d3 ♗e6 21 ♘c1 ♕a4 22 ♗xe7 ♖fc8 23 ♖d2 ♗c3 24 ♗xd6

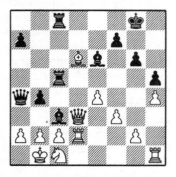

24...♗xa2+ 25 ♘xa2 ♖a5 26 ♔c1 ♕xa2 27 ♔d1 ♕xb2 28 ♗f4 ♗xd2 29 ♔xd2 ♖a3 White Resigns

What can we say about this game? Besides Black's devilish persistence in attack, we note that in such a sharp system White cannot afford to lose several tempi (e.g. 16 ♗h6 and then 17 ♗g5, as well as 19 ♕xd5 allowing ...♖c5) and still hope to come out ahead in the race.

In the Yugoslav Attack White will try to increase his offensive on the kingside by freeing his pieces from the defence of e4 by f2-f3 and then following up with h4, h5 (possibly including g4), hxg6, combined with ♗h6, the trade of Black's Dragon bishop and mate on the open or half-open h-file!

White's final assault is often prefaced by a decoy, sacrifice or exchange of the black knight on f6, when it remains the lone defender of the black king (see Karpov-Korchnoi, Dragon Game 6, below).

If White castles kingside and tries to attack with f4-f5 he relinquishes the e5 square to a black knight which uses it as a base to conduct both defence and counterattack.

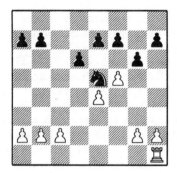

In the Dragon, a sound ...d5 is always a desirable lever for Black, but one which is very hard to achieve. Usually White has too much control of d5 or can follow with e5 which can quickly become unpleasant for Black. In some instances Black may, however, be able to achieve ...d5 by playing ...e5 first to drive a white piece from d4, and then quickly follow with ...d5.

The basis for Black's success in such instances is pressure on the half-open c-file, play on the potentially open d- and e-files, and pressure on White's pawn on e4.

DRAGON MASTERY LESSON 1

■ Exchanges tend to ease Black's defence in the Sicilian Defence

■ When White castles kingside and plays ♘b3 Black can use the manoeuvre ...♘a5 to facilitate exchanges

■ Later Black may use the manoeuvre ...♗e6, ...♗c4, to encourage further exchanges

■ Black can develop important central counterplay with the levers ...e5 and ...d5, supported by ...♖fd8

■ When Black's counterplay comes, it can be very dangerous for White as part of the "queenside-kingside swipe"

Dragon (Game 1)
V. Rauzer-M. Botvinnik
Leningrad 1933

When White castles kingside against the Dragon Black can sometimes generate particular activity. The following game by the late former World Champion, Mikhail Botvinnik, has been widely published so we present it here with few comments. Nevertheless it remains an outstanding example of Black playing ...e5, quickly followed by ...d5.

1 e4 c5 2 ♘f3 ♘c6 3 d4 cxd4 4 ♘xd4 ♘f6 5 ♘c3 d6 6 ♗e2 g6 7 ♗e3 ♗g7 8 ♘b3 ♗e6 9 f4 0-0 10 0-0 ♘a5

Usual now is 11 f5 ♗c4 12 ♗d3.

11 ♘xa5 ♕xa5

The exchange has exposed White's queenside and eased Black's game.

12 ♗f3 ♗c4

Very thematic.

13 ♖e1 ♖fd8 14 ♕d2 ♕c7 15 ♖ac1

White hopes to play b3 followed by ♘d5 and c4.

15...e5 16 b3

16...d5!!

Botvinnik has calculated sufficiently deeply to dash White's plans. Now on 17 bxc4 Black has

17...dxe4 recovering his piece with the better game. Other possibilities are:

(a) 17 ♘xd5 ♗xd5 18 exd5 e4! 19 ♗e2 ♘xd5 with advantage.

(b) 17 fxe5 ♘xe4 18 ♗xe4 dxe4 19 ♕f2 ♗xe5 and Black wins the h-pawn. Here play could continue 20 ♘xe4 ♗xh2+ 21 ♔h1 ♗e6 22 ♘f6+ ♔h8 23 ♗d4 with good play for White, but instead 19 ♕xe5 is an improvement.

17 exd5 e4! 18 bxc4 exf3 19 c5 ♕a5!

A very strong move which threatens another strong move, namely ...♘g4. Best for White now was simply 20 gxf3, but then 20...♘xd5 was unappealing.

20 ♖ed1 ♘g4 21 ♗d4 f2+

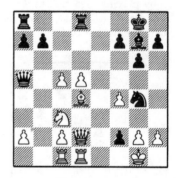

22 ♔f1

Not 22 ♔h1 ♖xd5! 23 ♘xd5 f1=♕+ winning.

22...♕a6+ 23 ♕e2 ♗xd4 24 ♖xd4 ♕f6 25 ♖cd1 ♕h4 26 ♕d3 ♖e8 27 ♖e4 f5 28 ♖e6 ♘xh2+ 29 ♔e2 ♕xf4

White resigned and Black received a brilliancy prize. Note again how all the fireworks began after ...e5 and ...d5. A truly exemplary Sicilian Dragon where both sides castled on the kingside.

DRAGON MASTERY LESSON 2

The Pseudo-Dragon

■ If White castles kingside and allows exchanges of minor pieces in the Dragon structure, while not making any effort to obtain the initiative, Black may quickly get the better game

■ Sources of Black's counterplay will often be on the half-open c-file, particularly via the c4 and c5 squares

■ Resulting endings may be easier for Black to play because of his long-term superior pawn structure

■ The exchange sacrifice ...♖xc3 may be used for a number of purposes, including the destruction of White's queenside pawn structure, to disrupt and seize the initiative, and for its sheer surprise value

Dragon (Game 2)
R.Nokes-D.Kopec
Edinburgh Congress 1981
Pseudo Dragon

When White plays against the Dragon without a particular plan, Black has few problems.

The following game illustrates that without the fireworks sparked by a sharp system of the Dragon, White will have difficulty obtaining the initiative.

1 e4 c5 2 ♘f3 ♘c6 3 d4 cxd4 4 ♘xd4 ♘f6 5 ♘c3 d6 6 ♗c4 ♗d7

Here Black initiates a system of which I am particularly fond—the Pseudo-Dragon Variation, a system so old as to be new to players who are under 40 years of age today!

Two good features of the Pseudo-Dragon Variation are:

(1) If White enters the race for attack by castling queenside then he'll discover that Black is actually in the lead.

(2) White has no chance of getting into the Yugoslav Attack. On the other hand Black must be ready to play against the Richter-Rauzer which will be discussed in the next chapter.

7 0-0 g6

Another important point is that if White now plays ♗e3, then Black has the strong reply ...♘g4. Here, 8 ♘xc6 is considered best for White, when on 8...♗xc6 9 ♘d5 Black cannot take the pawn by 9...♘xe4, because of 10 ♖e1.

8 f3 ♘xd4 9 ♕xd4 ♗g7 10 ♗e3 0-0 11 ♕d2 ♕c7 12 ♗e2 ♖fc8 13 ♖ac1 ♕a5

Since White has lost time with ♕d2, I figured that Black can afford to move his queen again. It is obvious that in this position Black has excellent play on the c-file.

14 ⅏fd1 ♗e6 15 ♗d4 a6 16 ♕e3 ♘d7

White does not seem to have any particular plan of attack so Black tries to improve his position by simplification. Naturally Black hopes for play along the half-open c-file and his fourth rank.

17 f4 ♗xd4 18 ♕xd4 ♕c5

Black continues his plan of simplification, and it becomes even more apparent that White has no attack.

19 ♗f3 ⅏ab8

Black prepares a dangerous minority attack on the queenside.

20 ♕xc5 ⅏xc5 21 g4

White's advance on the kingside is ill-advised since he will have to live with the weaknesses that he is creating. I could sense the desperation behind this move.

21...f6 22 a3 g5!

This move is excellent because it confirms the fact that the white bishop on f3 will be bad and the black knight will have a haven on e5.

23 e5

Again White takes desperate measures to avoid the aforementioned consequences of ...g5!.

23...fxe5 24 f5

This move does not help White. Better was simply 24 fxg5.

24...⅏xc3!?

A little impetuous, but Black wants to neutralise White's initiative. Nevertheless this exchange sacrifice is a recurring theme in Sicilians where Black is doing well. White has no open files for his rooks and very little pawn play.

25 bxc3 ♗c4 26 ⅏b1 b5 27 a4 ♘f6 28 ⅏e1 ⅏c8 29 ♗b7 ⅏c5 30 ♗xa6 bxa4 31 ♗xc4+ ⅏xc4 32 ⅏b4 ⅏xc3 33 ⅏xa4 ⅏xc2

Now it is clear that Black has all the winning chances.

34 ⅏b1 ♔f7 35 ⅏b7 e4 36 h3 e3 37 ⅏aa7 ♘d5 38 ⅏b3?

Better was 38 ⅏a1 but after ...♘f4 Black is clearly winning.

38...⅏c1+ 39 ♔g2 e2 0-1

DRAGON MASTERY LESSON 3

The Pseudo-Dragon

■ When White does not react aggressively to the Dragon Black can get an active game

■ After the exchange ♘xc6 bxc6 Black's centre is fortified and he can look forward to counterplay on the half-open b-file

■ After playing ...h6 and ...g5 Black should delay castling, but can continue active operations on the queenside and in the centre

■ It is important for Black to retain a grip on the key squares d5, e5, d4

■ When White does not play f4 or g3, the f4 square can be a pseudo-outpost

"Dragon" (Game 3)
P.Wolff-D.Kopec
St. John, New Brunswick, 1988

The following game is not a proper Dragon formation as Black is compelled to play an early ...h6 and ...g5, but it does illustrate many of the aspects of a successfully played Dragon including:

(1) queenside play for Black;

(2) control of critical central squares, partucularly e5;

(3) the ability to switch play from the queenside and centre to the kingside.

1 e4 c5 2 ♘f3 ♘c6 3 d4 cxd4 4 ♘xd4 ♘f6 5 ♘c3 d6 6 ♗c4 ♗d7

My favourite Pseudo-Dragon Variation. This choice of opening is ideal against Wolff who essentially is too young to know anything much about it—unless he has been following my games! At the time there were few databases, and *ChessBase* was just about making its appearance.

7 ♗e3 ♘g4 8 ♘xc6 bxc6

If 8...♘xe3?? 9 ♗xf7+ ♔xf7 10 ♕f3+.

9 ♗g5 h6 10 ♗h4 g5 11 ♗g3 ♗g7 12 ♕d2?

White misses what may be his only significant opportunity for improvement in the game: 12 ♕f3 0-0 13 h3 (13 h4 ♕a5) 13...♘e5 14 ♗xe5 ♗xe5—which is still viable for Black.

12...♘e5 13 ♗e2 ♖b8 14 ♘d1 ♕b6

If 14...h5?! 15 ♕xg5 ♗h6 16 ♕h4 (Davies).

15 0-0 ♗e6

Since Black has already weakened his kingside he does not want to castle. Instead he concentrates on queenside and central play.

16 c3 a5 17 ♕c2 ♘g6 18 ♔h1 ♕c5 19 f3 ♕b6 20 b3 h5

Obviously Black has gained significant space on both wings.

21 ♗f2 c5 22 ♘e3 ♗e5

Black's grip on the e5 and f4 squares is very imposing.

23 ♗c4 ♗d7!

A clever move for a number of reasons, but mainly because Black does not want to facilitate White's defensive task by exchanges. Black anticipates ♘d5 and prepares to gain control over that square with ...e6.

24 ♖ab1 ♕d8

And now Black envisages a shift of his queen to the kingside—possibly via f6.

25 ♗g1 h4

Throughout the game Black emphasizes his grip on the dark squares.

26 a3 ♘f4 27 b4

Better was 27 ♖fd1 ♘h5 28 ♗f2 (Davies).

27...axb4 28 cxb4 ♘h5 29 ♗f2 cxb4 30 ♖xb4

30...♘g3+ 31 hxg3 hxg3+ 32 ♔g1 gxf2+ 33 ♔xf2

Finally the white king is exposed and he will miss the absence of his dark-squared bishop.

33...♖xb4 34 axb4 ♕b6

And now the black queen returns for the decisive queenside-kingside swipe.

35 ♔e2 ♖h2 36 ♕a2 e6!

This little pawn move provides a safe haven for the black king on e7, while also stopping ♘d5.

37 ♕a5 ♕d4

Naturally, on seeing the possibility of this incursion, Black rejects the trade of queens.

38 ♖d1 ♖xg2+! 39 ♔f1 0-1

White resigns, recognizing that Black has a number of winning choices, including ...♖d2 and ...♕xe3, e.g., 39...♕xe3 40 ♔xg2 g4! and the white king is quite helpless against the assault which is to follow. If 39 ♘xg2, the basic idea behind the combination is 39...♕xc4+ 40 ♔f2 (40 ♖d3 ♗b5 41 ♘e1 g4) 40...♕c2+ 41 ♔e1 ♗c3+.

DRAGON MASTERY LESSON 4

The Pseudo-Dragon

■ **When White plays 8 ♘xc6 against the Pseudo-Dragon he is assured of at least a small but clear advantage**

■ **After Black is forced to capture ♗xd5 exd5 he should seek counterplay on the queenside with ...b5**

■ **You can sometimes be a pawn down and draw due to the activity of your forces in the ending**

Dragon (Game 4)
Iversland-D.Kopec
North Atlantic Correspondence
Team Tournament, 1992-1994

The following game illustrates how play might go when White is familiar with the best theoretical continuation against the Pseudo-Dragon Variation.

1 e4 c5 2 ♘f3 ♘c6 3 d4 cxd4 4 ♘xd4 ♘f6 5 ♘c3 d6 6 ♗c4 ♗d7 7 0-0 g6 8 ♘xc6 ♗xc6

This is considered better than 8...bxc6 as occurred in Gilden-Kopec, US Open, 1974, which continued 9 f4 ♕b6+ 10 ♔h1 ♘g4 11 ♕e2 ♗g7 12 e5 (if 12 h3 h5!? is possible) d5 13 ♗d3 ♘h6 14 ♗e3 d4 15 ♗g1 0-0 16 ♘e4 c5 17 c3 ♘f5 18 b4 cxb4 19 cxd4 ♖ac8 20 ♘c5 ♗c6 21 ♗xf5 ? gxf5 22 ♕h5 e6 23 ♗e3 ♗d5 24 ♔g1 ♕c6 Drawn, although Black is better in the final position.

9 ♘d5

Now Black cannot play 9...♘xe4? because of 10 ♖e1 with a decisive advantage.

9...♗g7 10 ♗g5 ♗xd5 11 exd5 0-0 12 ♖e1

White has a small advantage due to the half-open e-file and his pressure against the backward e-pawn.

12...♖e8 13 ♗b5 ♖f8 14 c4 a6 15 ♗a4 ♖b8 16 ♖c1 b5 17 ♗b3 ♖b7 18 cxb5 axb5 19 ♖c6 ♕d7 20 ♕c2 ♕g4 21 ♗d2 ♕d7 22 h3

Throughout White has retained a small but undeniable advantage.

22...♖e8 23 ♗b4 ♗h6 24 ♗c3 ♗g7 25 a3 ♕d8 26 ♕e2 ♘d7

Black hopes to reach a simplified position in which his knight is a better piece than the black bishop.

27 ♗xg7 ♔xg7 28 ♖xd6

White wins a pawn but Black has seen deeply into an ending in which his knight will be more active than the white bishop, thereby providing adequate compensation for the pawn deficit.

28...exd6 29 ♕xe8 ♕xe8 30 ♖xe8 b4 31 ♖e3 ♘c5 32 ♗c4 bxa3 33 bxa3 f5 34 g3 ♔f6 35 f4 h6

Black's position is very compact and active.

36 ♔g2 ½-½

DRAGON MASTERY LESSON 5

The Double-Fianchetto Setup

■ **When White castles kingside Black has a number of setups**

■ **Black may employ a double-fianchetto coupled with ...a5 and ...b6 when White castles kingside**

■ **Sources of Black's counterplay will often be on the half-open c-file, particularly via the c4 and c5 squares, and sometimes the e5 square when White plays f5**

■ **Black can use a "preventive" defence with a knight going to d7 and c5**

■ **Black's queen's knight can sometimes find counterplay via the ...b4 square**

Dragon (Game 5)
D.London–D.Kopec
New York 1983

1 e4

This was the last round of a New York international all-play-all tournament in which I scored my first official IM norm. In order to achieve this I had to score two points from the last three rounds. And it all came down to this game which I needed to win as Black. I devised an opening strategy which

was aimed at frustrating the aggressive predilections of my opponent, who was known for his attacking play.

1...c5 2 ♘f3 ♘c6 3 d4 cxd4 4 ♘xd4 ♘f6 5 ♘c3 d6 6 ♗e2

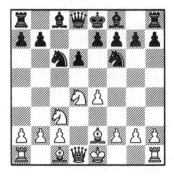

This move is not as aggressive as 6 ♗c4 (when I would play the Pseudo-Dragon, 6...♗d7) or 6 ♗g5, the Richter Rauzer. And so, since White is not playing the most aggressive setup, I thought this would be an opportunity to play the Dragon. Right or wrong, it was important that I was thinking right from the start.

6...g6 7 0-0 ♗g7 8 ♘b3 0-0 9 ♗g5

A rather aggressive deployment, not usually played by White against the Dragon. Hence my choice of continuation.

9...a5 10 a4 b6

Despite the hole on b5, I am already playing for ...♘d7 and ...♘c5.

11 f4 ♗b7 12 ♗f3 h6 13 ♗h4 ♘b4

Aimed against ♘d5 or e5 and trying to get White to exercise restraint.

14 ♖f2 ♕c8 15 ♖d2 ♖e8 16 ♗f2 ♕b8 17 ♔h1 ♘d7 18 ♘d4 ♘c5

Black has some pressure on White's centre and may even be able to play ...e5 at an opportune moment.

19 f5 ♘c6 20 ♘xc6 ♗xc6 21 ♘d5 ♖a7

Continuing with rock-solid play.

22 e5

White tries to develop some play but Black's setup is very solid.

22...♗xe5 23 fxg6 fxg6 24 ♘xe7+ ♖axe7 25 ♗xc6 ♖f8 26 c3

Black's activity fully compensates for his slightly weakened pawn structure.

26...♔h7 27 ♗g1 ♖ef7 28 ♕e2

It's hard to tell if White has just blundered or was simply unnerved by Black's activity.

28...♘b3 29 ♖ad1 ♘xd2 30 ♖xd2 ♖f4

After this gain of material, Black concentrates on remaining both active and solid.

31 g3 ♖f1 32 ♔g2 ♕c8 33 ♗e4 ♕e8 34 ♗xb6 ♕xa4

Black's queen has an influence on many regions of the board.

35 ♕g4 ♕e8 36 ♗xa5 ♕f7

Now there are numerous threats, including ...♖a1.

37 ♗b6 ♔g7 38 ♗e3 ♖f6 39 ♗d5 ♕e8 40 ♕h4 g5 41 ♕e4 ♕h5

Black probes for an entry square on the kingside.

42 h3 ♖e8 43 ♗c6 ♖ef8 44 ♕g4 ♕g6

Black estimates that victory will come more easily with queens on the board.

45 ♗e4 ♕e8 46 h4 ♗f4!

Suddenly White's weaknesses are exposed.

47 ♕f3 ♗xg3 48 ♗c6 ♖xf3 49 ♗d4+ ♗e5 50 ♗xe8 ♗xd4

Black has a decisive material advantage.

0-1

DRAGON MASTERY LESSON 6

Opposite Wing Attacks

■ When White and Black castle on the queenside and kingside, respectively, play becomes very aggressive and a race to attack will typically ensue

■ White pursues chances on the h-file with h4-h5 while Black seeks counterplay by ...♘c4, ...b5, ...a5, etc;

■ The move ♘de2 is one of White's primary defensive motifs

■ A number of ideas involving the sacrifice of the exchange by Black for a continuing initiative and/or weakening of the white king may follow

■ Earlier, ♗h6 was the more popular way for White to proceed

■ Today, ♗g5 with pressure on Black through the centre is more popular

Dragon (Game 6)
A.Karpov-V.Korchnoi
Candidates Match, Moscow 1974

In the 1970s it was very common for White to play the Yugoslav Attack (with f3, ♗c4, 0-0-0, h4, h5 etc.) and both sides would race to attack each other's kings. White usually won those races and this game is just one such example of many—with a few subtle touches.

1 e4 c5 2 ♘f3 d6 3 d4 cxd4 4 ♘xd4 ♘f6 5 ♘c3 g6 6 ♗e3 ♗g7 7 f3 ♘c6 8 ♕d2 0-0 9 ♗c4 ♗d7 10 h4 ♖c8 11 ♗b3 ♘e5 12 0-0-0 ♘c4 13 ♗xc4 ♖xc4 14 h5 ♘xh5 15 g4 ♘f6 16 ♘de2 ♕a5 17 ♗h6

17...♗xh6

An interesting try for Black is 17... ♗h8, and, although after 18 ♗xf8 ♔xf8 19 ♔b1 Black generates some play, White has come out ahead more often, e.g., 18 ♗xf8 ♔xf8 19 ♔b1 (19 ♕e3 ♖c5 20 ♘d4 ♗e6 21 ♔b1 b5 22 ♘xe6+ fxe6 winning, Kruppa-Golubev, USSR 1984) 19...♖b4 (Other tries here are: (a) 19...♗e6 20 ♘f4 g5 21 ♘xe6+ fxe6 22 ♘e2 ♕e5 23 c3 ♗g7 24 ♘c1 h6 25 ♘d3 ♕b5 26 ♖he1 Chudinovskih-Yakmimainen, USSR 1977; and (b) 19...♗g7 20 ♘d5 ♕a6 21 ♘xf6 ♗xf6 22 ♖xh7 ♗e6 23 ♘f4 ♕b5 24 ♘xe6+ fxe6 25 ♕h6+ ♔e8 26 ♕xg6+ winning, Cuijpers-Kaspret, Dortmund 1980) 20 g5, when one continuation leading to an unclear position is 20...♘h5 21 ♘c1 ♗e6 22 ♘b3 ♕e5 23 ♖xh5 ♗xb3 24 ♖xh7 ♗xa2+ 25 ♔c1 ♗g7 26 ♖dh1 Almrot-Gernud, corres 1974. Another 17th move for

Black is 17...♖fc8 18 ♗xg7 ♔xg7 19 ♕h6+ (transposing into Karpov-Korchnoi) 19...♔g8 20 ♖d5 (20 ♖d3 ♗e6 21 g5 ♘h5 22 ♘g3 ♕e5 23 ♘xh5 gxh5 24 ♕xh5 ♕g7 25 f4 d5 26 ♖hd1 with unclear play, Zambon-Wagman, Italy 1974). A game which ended quickly in White's favour, continued 20...♕d8 21 e5 dxe5 22 ♖d2 (or 22 g5 ♘h5 23 ♘g3 ♕f8!, when after 24 ♘xh5 ♕xh6 25 gxh6 ♗c6! Black is better; or if instead 23 ♖xh5 gxh5 24 ♖xd6 ♕xh6 25 gxh6 and Black is not worse) 22...♕e8 23 ♘d5 ♗e6 24 ♘xf6+ exf6 25 g5 fxg5 26 ♕xh7+ Prandstetter-Spiridonov, Agard 1976.

18 ♕xh6 ♖fc8

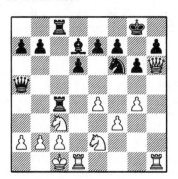

19 ♖d3

This may be the star move of the game, the main feature of which is the overprotection of c3.

After 19 g5 one spectacular continuation is 19...♘h5 20 ♖xh5 gxh5 21 ♘d5 ♖xc2+ 22 ♔b1 ♕d8 23 ♘ef4 ♕f8 24 ♘xe7+ ♕xe7 25 ♘d5 ♖xb2+ 26 ♔xb2 ± Dobsa-Reinhardt, corres. 1982.

Another continuation is 19 ♖d5 ♖8c5 (perhaps best is 19...♕d8(!) 20 e5 dxe5 (20 g5 ♘h5 21 ♘g3 ♕f8 22 ♕xf8+ ♖xf8! 23 ♘xh5

gxh5 24 ♖xh5 f5! when "Black has a nice position" Speelman, in *Best Chess Games 1970-1980*, p.126) 21 ♖d2 ♕c7 22 ♘d5 ♖xc2+ 23 ♔b1 ♖xd2 24 ♘xc7 ♖xe2 25 ♘d5 ♖e8 26 ♘c3 was unclear in Omelchenko-Mikhailov, World Correspondence Championship 1977. After 19 ♖d5 ♕c7? 20 ♔b1 ♔h8 White won quickly in Skjoldager-Dalhoff, corres. 1975). Instead, after 19 ♖d5 ♖8d5 20 ♖xc5 ♖xc5 21 ♘d5 ♖xd5 22 exd5 ♕xd5 23 ♖h3 ♕xa2 24 b3 ♕a1+ 25 ♔d2 ♕f1 26 ♖g3, the game was unclear in Ipek-Eskelinen, Groningen 1982.

19...♖4c5 20 g5 ♖xg5 21 ♖d5!

This is the key interference/decoy of this game.

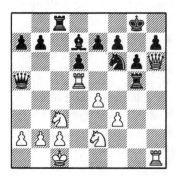

21...♖xd5 22 ♘xd5 ♖e8 23 ♘ef4 ♗c6 24 e5!

The interference theme is repeated with devastating and beautiful effect.

24...♗xd5

If 24...♘xd5 25 ♘h5 and White wins.

25 exf6 exf6 26 ♕xh7+ ♔f8 27 ♕h8+ 1-0

The end could be 27...♔e7 28 ♘xd5+ ♕xd5 29 ♖e1+.

A typically eclectic and sharp victory for White in the Dragon.

DRAGON MASTERY LESSON 7

Opposite Wing Attacks

■ When White and Black castle on the queenside and kingside, respectively, play becomes very aggressive and a race to attack will typically ensue

■ White pursues chances on the h-file with h4-h5 while Black seeks counterplay with ...♘c4, ...b5, ...a5, etc

■ When White wins the black b-pawn Black retains counterplay on the half-open b-file

■ In certain specific circumstances Black may be able to play ...♗xc3 to destroy the pawn position in front of the white king and retain long-term attacking chances

■ The lever ...d5 for Black may always become a dangerous rejoinder

---

Dragon (Game 7)
N.Short-V.Topalov
Linares 1995

This game shows how defensive techniques for Black have improved over the past twenty years...

1 e4 c5 2 ♘f3 d6 3 d4 cxd4 4 ♘xd4 ♘f6 5 ♘c3 g6 6 ♗e3 ♗g7

Of course now 6...♘g4? is met by 7 ♗b5+.

7 f3 ♘c6 8 ♕d2 0-0 9 ♗c4 ♗d7 10 0-0-0 ♘e5 11 ♗b3 ♖c8

12 g4

The text is considered second-best because White is a tempo behind in certain race variations. The "fastest" line is 12 h4 ♕a5 (or ♕c7) 13 ♔b1, when in the ensuing sharp continuations Black does not seem to have enough to equalize. This is also true after 12 h4 ♘c4 13 ♗xc4 ♖xc4 14 h5 when great complications follow, not unfavourable for White (as in Dragon Mastery Game 6 above).

One variation credited to GM Andrew Soltis is 12 h4 h5 13 ♗h6 ♗xh6 14 ♕xh6 ♖xc3 15 bxc3 (see Dragon Mastery Game 8 below).

12...b5

Besides attacking, this move takes advantage of the fact that the white knight on d4 is tied to the defence of f3.

13 g5 ♘h5 14 ♘cxb5

Now instead of equalizing material, Topalov finds a strong way to exploit his half-open files on the queenside.

14...♘c4 15 ♗xc4 ♖xc4 16 ♕d3 ♖b4

Now 17 a3 is met by ...♗xb5, while on 17 c3 Black has ...♖a4.

17 ♘c3 ♕b8 18 ♘b3

18 b3 was recommended by Yasser Seirawan, when Black still has to prove compensation for the pawn.

18...♗e6

Directed against ♘d5 but also preparing ...a5.

19 ♕a6 ♗xc3 20 bxc3 ♖b7

Now Black threatens ...♖c8.

21 ♖d4 ♖c8 22 ♔d2 ♕c7 23 ♕d3

23...d5!

An unexpected rejoinder, typical of the fierce struggle to retain the initiative in Sicilians with attacks on opposite wings. The main idea of this shot is to open both the f5 square for Black's bishop and also the b8-h2 diagonal. Black cannot play 23...♗c4 24 ♖xc4 ♕xc4 25 ♕xc4 ♖xc4 26 ♘a5, winning back the exchange.

24 ♔c1 dxe4 25 fxe4 ♗c4 26 ♕d2 e5! 27 ♖d6 ♘f4

All of Black's forces are in play.

28 ♗xf4 exf4 29 ♖d1 f3

Black prepares for the endgame.

30 ♕f4 ♕e7

31 ♕xf3 ♕xg5+ favours Black.

31 h4 ♗e2 32 ♖1d5 ♖bc7 33 ♘d4 ♗c4

Not 33 ♖xc3?! 34 ♖d7 with dangerous counterplay.

34 ♕xf3 ♗xd5 35 ♖xd5 ♖xc3 36 ♕f6 ♕c7 37 ♕f2 ♕c4 38 ♔b2 ♕b4+ 39 ♔a1 ♖h3 40 ♕g2 ♖e3 0-1.

An excellent attacking game.

Dragon (Game 8)
C.Pritchett-A.Soltis
Haifa 1970

1 e4 c5 2 ♘f3 d6 3 d4 cxd4 4 ♘xd4 ♘f6 5 ♘c3 g6 6 ♗e3 ♗g7 7 f3 ♘c6 8 ♕d2 0-0 9 ♗c4 ♗d7 10 h4 h5 11 0-0-0 ♖c8 12 ♗b3 ♘e5 13 ♗h6 ♗xh6 14 ♕xh6 ♖xc3 15 bxc3

The main moves in this position are 15...♕a5 and 15...♕c7. A wild but unsuccessful attempt to refute the line could go:

15...♕a5

16 ♕e3

If 16 f4 ♘fg4 17 ♕g5 ♕xc3 18 fxe5 ♕a1+ 19 ♔d2 ♕xd4+ 20 ♔c1 ♕xe5 21 ♕xg6+ ♕g7 22 ♕xg7+ ♔xg7 and Black has excellent play for the exchange thanks to the possibility of his knight taking up residence on e5. *BCO II* gives 16 ♔b1! ♖c8 17 g4 ♕xc3 18 gxh5 ♘c4 (18...♘xh5 occurred in Grunfeld-Findlay, Toronto, 1984, and continued 19 ♖hg1 ♘c4 20 ♗xc4 ♖xc4 21 ♕xh5 ♖xd4 22 ♖xg6+ when White wins thanks to mate or win of the rook on d4) 19 ♗xc4 ♖xc4 20 ♖d3 ♕b4+ 21 ♘b3 ♘xh5 with a slight advantage for White.

16...♖c8 17 ♔b2 ♕b6

The unpleasant ...a5 is threatened. This is typical probing by Black in the Soltis Variation. Due to his weakened queenside pawn structure, White can do little to demonstrate an initiative, even in an ending.

18 ♔a1 ♕c5 19 g4 a5 20 gxh5 ♘xh5 21 ♕h6 a4

Rarely is a capture with check a bad thing, so 21...♕xc3+ also wins.

22 ♗xf7+ ♔xf7 23 ♕h7+ ♘g7 24 ♘e2 ♕c4 25 h5 ♗e6 26 hxg6+ ♘xg6 27 ♔b1 ♖h8

Or 27...♕xa2+ 28 ♔c1 ♗b3.

28 ♕xg6+ ♔xg6 29 ♖dg1+ ♔f7 30 ♖xh8 ♕b5+ 31 ♔c1 ♕xe2 0-1

DRAGON MASTERY LESSON 9

The Soltis Variation: Opposite Wing Attack with ...♖xc3

■ When White and Black castle on the queenside and kingside, respectively, play becomes very aggressive and a race to attack will typically ensue

■ White pursues chances on the h-file with h4 while Black may try to slow the attack down with ...h5

■ A number of ideas involving the sacrifice of the exchange by Black with ... ♖xc3 (the Soltis Variation) for a continuing initiative and/or weakening of the white king may follow

■ Always look for central breaks with ...d5 for Black, especially when White neutralizes Black's play on the queenside in the Soltis Variation

Dragon (Game 9)
B.Spassky-J.Mestel
London 1982

The following game shows another side of the coin where the Soltis Variation is not entirely successful. It pitted a renowned Dragon expert, GM Jonathan Mestel, against a renowned player: former World Champion Boris Spassky. However, I ask the reader to consider whether the variation fails, or Black's play was sub-par.

1 e4 c5 2 ♘f3 d6 3 d4 cxd4 4 ♘xd4 ♘f6 5 ♘c3 g6 6 ♗e3 ♗g7 7 f3 0-0 8 ♕d2 ♘c6 9 ♗c4 ♗d7 10 h4 ♖c8 11 ♗b3 h5 12 0-0-0 ♘e5 13 ♗h6 ♗xh6 14 ♕xh6 ♖xc3 15 bxc3 ♕a5 16 ♔b2 ♖c8 17 ♕d2 ♕b6 18 ♔a1 a5 19 a3 ♕c5 20 ♔b2

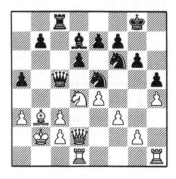

Play is "normal" to here and indeed it is important for Black to come up with some sort of plan otherwise White will indeed be better thanks to his material advantage. However, I simply ask what is wrong with 20...d5! in this position? I think this move will lead to tremendous counterplay for Black. I can't imagine what White might do after, for example, the following: 20...d5 21 exd5 ♘xd5 22 ♘e2 ♘e3 etc.

20...♗e8 21 ♖h3 ♕b6 22 ♔a1 ♕c5 23 ♔b2 a4 24 ♗a2 ♘c4+ 25 ♗xc4 ♕xc4 26 ♖g3 ♔h7 27 ♕d3 ♕c5 28 f4 ♘d7 29 ♘f3 ♘b6 30 ♘d2 e5 31 f5 ♖c6 32 ♖f1 ♔g7 33 ♕f3 ♕b5+ 34 ♔c1 ♕c5 35 fxg6 ♕xa3+ 36 ♔d1 f5 37 ♕xf5 ♘d7 38 ♕e6 d5 39 ♖f7+ 1-0

Dragon (Game 10)
V.Anand-G.Kasparov
World Championship,
New York 1995

1 e4 c5 2 ♘f3 d6 3 d4 cxd4 4 ♘xd4 ♘f6 5 ♘c3 g6

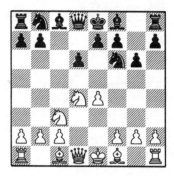

This was the the first time that Kasparov elected to play the Dragon in a serious game. Previously, he had only tried the Accelerated Dragon (1 e4 c5 2 ♘f3 ♘c6 3 d4 cxd4 4 ♘xd4 g6) against Fritz in an exhibition game. This decision to play the Dragon turned out brilliantly. Anand was not prepared for it and was unable to pose any problems for Kasparov, particularly because he did not enter any of the difficult theoretical discussions in the Dragon until he had already lost twice against it.

6 ♗e3 ♗g7 7 f3 0-0 8 ♕d2 ♘c6 9 ♗c4

As White, against Bulgarian GM Veselin Topalov at the Euwe Memorial, Kasparov preferred 9 0-0-0.

9...♗d7 10 0-0-0 ♘e5 11 ♗b3 ♖c8 12 h4 h5 13 ♔b1 ♘c4 14 ♗xc4 ♖xc4 15 ♘de2 b5

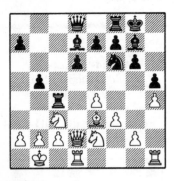

16 ♗h6

This is not the most common move in this position today, and has been supplanted by the more "pressure-based" 16 ♗g5.

An early game, (Liberzon-Miles, Haifa 1976) continued 16 e5 dxe5 17 ♗g5 ♖c7 18 ♗xf6 exf6 19 g4 ♕e8 20 gxh5 ♗e6 21 ♖dg1 b4 22 ♘e4 f5 23 h6 fxe4 24 hxg7 ♔xg7

25 h5 ♗xa2+ 26 ♔xa2 ♕a4+ 27 ♔b1 ♖d8 28 ♕xd8 ♕xc2+ 29 ♔a1 ♕a4+ ½-½, although since then improvements have been found for both sides.

16...♕a5

This is not a theoretical novelty—it was previously played in Suetin-Szabo, Leningrad 1967, but it is very rare. Attention has mainly been focused on 16...b4, with the most important game involving one of Anand's seconds, Patrick Wolff, against K.Georgiev, Biel, 1993, which went 17 ♗xg7 ♔xg7 18 ♘d5 ♘xd5 19 exd5 ♕a5 20 b3 ♖c5 21 g4 ♖fc8 22 ♕d4+ ♔g8 23 ♖d2 hxg4 24 fxg4 e5 25 dxe6 ♗xe6 26 ♘f4 ♖e5 27 ♘d3 ♕d5 28 ♕xd5 ♖xd5 29 g5 a5 30 ♖hh2 ♔f8 31 ♔b2 ♔e7 32 a3 bxa3+ 33 ♔xa3 ♖h8 with a draw in 47 moves.

17 ♗xg7 ♔xg7 18 ♘f4 ♖fc8 19 ♘cd5

White opts to simplify as he has no attacking chances. Kasparov mentioned more than once after the game that "White has no real chances for an advantage in the Dragon if he doesn't play g2-g4."

19...♕xd2

Kasparov offered a draw after making his move.

20 ♖xd2

Anand thought for four minutes before declining the draw, the first time in the match that an offer had been refused. During the press conference Garry compared this encounter with the 47th game of his epic first match with Anatoly Karpov.

20...♘xd5 21 ♘xd5 ♚f8 22 ♖e1 ♖b8

A mysterious rook move. More direct was 22...♗e6.

23 b3 ♖c5 24 ♘f4 ♖bc8 25 ♚b2 a5 26 a3 ♚g7 27 ♘d5 ♗e6

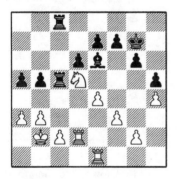

28 b4?

Losing the thread. But what about 28 ♘xe7? Kasparov rattled off the following variation at the post-game press conference: 28 ♘xe7 ♖e8 29 ♘d5 ♗xd5 30 b4 axb4 31 axb4 ♖c4 32 ♖xd5 ♖ec8 33 ♖e2 ♖xb4+ 34 ♚c1 ♖c6 35 ♖ed2 ♖a6! 36 ♚d1 ♖b1+.

However after 28 ♘xe7 Wolff countered Kasparov's analysis with the following: 28...♖e8 29 b4 ♖c4 30 ♘d5 ♗xd5 31 ♖xd5 axb4 32 axb4 (a) On 32...♖ec8 (Kasparov) 33 c3! (Wolff's suggestion instead

of 33 ♖e2) 33...♖xc3 34 ♖e2 ± (Wolff); or on (b) 32...♖xb4+ 33 ♚c3 ♖c4+ 34 ♚b3 ♖ec8 35 ♖e2 decides (Wolff). So it seems that the burden of proof after 28 ♘xe7 lies on Kasparov's shoulders. Interestingly, at this very moment, Anand falls for a little combinational trap prepared by his opponent.

28...axb4 29 axb4 ♖c4 30 ♘b6??

A horrible hallucination. Here White had to try 30 ♘xe7, though 30...♖xb4+ 31 ♚c1 ♗a2 32 ♖xd6 ♖b1+ 33 ♚d2 ♖xc2+ 34 ♚xc2 ♖xe1 leaves Black with winning chances.

30...♖xb4+ 31 ♚a3

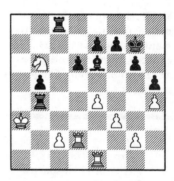

31...♖xc2!!

The move Anand overlooked! But such an oversight is quite plausible when your defences are down.

Anand resigned here, seeing the following continuation: 31...♖xc2 32 ♖xc2 (32 ♚xb4 ♖xd2 winning) 32...♖b3+ 33 ♚a2 ♖e3+ 34 ♚b2 ♖xe1 winning. From this point on in the match it was easy to see that Anand was demoralized and had lost much of his fighting spirit.

DRAGON MASTERY LESSON 11

White King caught in Centre

■ Exchanges tend to ease Black's defence in the Sicilian Defence

■ If White strengthens Black's centre with moves like ♘xc6 and does not seek an initiative, Black may seize the initiative himself by natural means including exploitation of half-open files and levers

■ Black may use the manoeuvre ...♗e6 to unsettle a white bishop on c4 or b3. The capture ♗xe6 and recapture ...fxe6 is not usually dangerous for Black

Dragon (Game 11)
V.Anand-G.Kasparov
World Championship,
New York 1995

This game again illustrates that if White does not play actively against the Dragon Variation, Black will have excellent chances right into the middlegame.

1 e4 c5 2 ♘f3 d6 3 d4 cxd4 4 ♘xd4 ♘f6 5 ♘c3 g6

A repeat of the Dragon came as a bit of a surprise for the Grandmasters in the press room. They expected a return to the Najdorf/Scheveningen seen in games 1,3,5,7, and 9.

6 ♗e3 ♗g7 7 ♕d2

Vishy played the normal Yugo-slav Attack move order in Game 11 (7 f3 and 8 ♕d2), but here he offers Garry the opportunity to mix things up with 7... ♘g4 8 ♗b5+ ♔f8.

7...♘c6 8 f3 0-0 9 ♗c4 ♗d7 10 h4

Game 11 saw 10 0-0-0 ♘e5 11 ♗b3 ♖c8 12 h4 h5 13 ♔b1. The text looks like it will transpose, but Anand has a surprise in store.

10...h5 11 ♗b3 ♖c8

12 ♘xc6

A little known and unorthodox way of handling the Yugoslav Attack. However, it has little to recommend it. Black's centre is strengthened and he gains natural play from its advance while retaining chances on the half-open b-file.

12...bxc6 13 ♗h6 c5 14 ♗c4

An alternative recommended by Grandmaster commentator Roman Dzindzichashvili is 14 ♗xg7 ♔xg7 15 ♕e2, believing that the resulting position favours White. This was tried out in Madl-Farago, Budapest 1989 where White held the advantage after 15...♕c7 16 ♗c4.

14...♕b6

Kasparov is the first to vary. Tolnai-Watson, Kecskemet, 1988,

saw 14...♖b8 15 0-0-0 ♖b4 16 ♗b3
♕c7 17 ♗xg7 ♔xg7 18 a3 ♖d4
with unclear play. Neither player
seemed to be familiar with this
game.

15 ♗xg7 ♔xg7 16 b3?!

White's delay in castling only
precipitates the forthcoming trouble.
He should play 16 0-0-0 ♖b8 17 b3
♕a5 18 ♔b2 ♖b4 19 ♘d5 ♘xd5 20
exd5 when he still has an edge.

16...♗e6!

An important and old motif in
such simplified Dragon positions.
The removal of White's c4-bishop
is more important than the damage
to Black's pawn structure. Once the
white bishop is removed from its
perch on c4, Black can advance
with c4 and achieve counterplay.
World Champion Kasparov's
familiarity with this motif is to be
expected. A sample continuation
might be 17 ♗xe6!? fxe6 18 0-0-0
c4 19 g4 cxb3 20 axb3 ♕a5 21 ♔b2
hxg4 and Black has good chances of
enduring White's play on the kingside while mounting a counterattack
on the c-file.

17 ♘d5 ♗xd5 18 exd5

18...e5

The right way to advance. Here
the natural-looking 18...e6 would
have been met not by 19 dxe6, but
19 0-0-0, when Black has nothing
better than 19...e5.

19 dxe6??

In the post-game press conference, Kasparov criticized this move
preferring 19 0-0-0, when he said
the position would be about equal.

19...d5 20 ♗e2 c4

After the game, Kasparov re-
marked that this was, "the first time
in my life that I prevented castling
on two wings with one move."
With 20...c4 kingside castling is
rendered illegal and queenside
castling undesirable.

21 c3

The losing move. Forced was 21
♖d1, planning ♕d4 and making
♖d2 available. The text loses almost
instantly. Kasparov gave 21 ♖d1 c3
22 ♕d4 fxe6 as slightly better for
Black (23 ♕e5 ♕c7).

21...♖ce8

Not an easy move to find. The
rook is already well-developed but

all the action is occurring on the e-file.

22 bxc4

Alternatives fare no better. Kasparov gave the following pretty variations in the VIP room: 21 exf7 ♖xf7 22 ♖f1 ♖fe7 23 ♖f2 ♖xe2+ 24 ♖xe2 ♕g1 mate and 21 exf7 ♖xf7 22 ♔d1 ♖fe7 23 ♖e1 d4 24 cxd4 ♘d5 and Black's knight decisively enters the attack.

22...♖xe6 23 ♔f1 ♖fe8 24 ♗d3 dxc4 25 ♗xc4

In this short game, the poor white bishop has moved no less than six times!

25...♘e4 0-1

After 26 fxe4 ♖f6+ 27 ♔e1 ♖xe4+ 28 ♗e2 ♕f2+ 29 ♔d1 ♖xe2 Black wins.

After the next to last draw in Game 8, the match had become a slugfest with decisive results in four of the last five games. Unfortunately for Anand, it was the Champion who was throwing most of the punches.

Kasparov's press comments and notes are based on those published by GM Yasser Seirawan in *Inside Chess*, 1995, No. 21, p.8-9.

DRAGON MASTERY LESSON 12

Positional Pressure towards a Superior Ending

■ When White and Black castle on the queenside and kingside, respectively, play becomes very aggressive and a race to attack will typically ensue

■ White pursues chances on the h-file with h4-h5, then possibly g4, while Black seeks counterplay with ...♘c4, ...b5, ...a5, etc

■ Recent theory has White opting for positional pressure with ♗g5 and later possibly ♘d5 in hope of a superior ending

■ White must exploit endgame advantages carefully

Dragon (Game 12)
V.Anand-G.Kasparov
World Championship,
New York 1995

Finally Anand took Kasparov on in a main theoretical variation of the Dragon. One wonders why it took him so long to do so, as he certainly had winning chances in this game.

1 e4 c5 2 ♘f3 d6 3 d4 cxd4 4 ♘xd4 ♘f6 5 ♘c3 g6 6 ♗e3 ♗g7 7 f3 0-0 8 ♕d2 ♘c6 9 ♗c4 ♗d7 10 h4 h5 11 ♗b3 ♖c8 12 0-0-0 ♘e5 13 ♗g5

This is considered the main theoretical line (rather than ♗h6). White prepares f4 followed by e5 as well as possible pressure on e7 after the exchange which follows ♘d5 exd5.

13...♖c5

And this is Black's standard reply, restraining e5 and preparing ...b5.

14 ♔b1 ♖e8?

A waiting move, hard to comprehend. Normal is ...b5 and then ...a5.

15 ♖he1 ♕a5 16 a3

Another waiting move to see how Black intends to improve (or further weaken) his position. An earlier game went 16 f4 ♘c4 17 ♗xc4 ♖xc4 18 ♗xf6 ♗xf6 19 ♘d5 ♕xd2 20 ♘xf6+ exf6 21 ♖xd2 f5 22 b3 ♖c3 23 ♖d3 ♖xd3 24 cxd3 fxe4 25 dxe4 ♗f5 26 ♘xf5 gxf5 27 e5 ½-½, Beliavsky-Kir.Georgiev, Wijk aan Zee 1985.

16...b5 17 ♗xf6 exf6

Since ♘d5 and ♘xf6+ would follow anyway, Black elects to keep both his bishops. However his damaged pawn structure will soon prove to be a liability.

18 ♘de2 ♖c6 19 ♘d5 ♕xd2 20 ♖xd2 ♘c4

Essentially this move allows White to liquidate to an advantageous position. Better was 20...♔f8.

21 ♗xc4 bxc4 22 ♖ed1 f5 23 exf5

On 23 ♘b4 ♖b6 24 ♖xd6 ♖xd6 25 ♖xd6 fxe4 26 fxe4 (26 ♖xd7 exf3!) ♗g4 Black has no problems.

23...♗xf5 24 ♘d4 ♗xd4 25 ♖xd4 ♖e2 26 ♖4d2 ♖xd2 27 ♖xd2 ♔f8

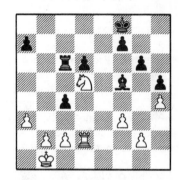

Black's fragmented pawn structure indicates a definite advantage for White.

28 ♔c1?

Anand misses an important opportunity with 28 ♘b4! ♖b6 (28...c3 29 ♖d5 ♖c4 30 g3! ♔e7 31 ♖a5 winning. Now 31...♖c7 cannot be played because of 32 ♘d5+. (Seirawan)) 29 ♖d5! ♗c8 30 ♖a5 a6 31 ♔c1 ♖b5 32 ♖xb5 axb5 33 ♔d2 ♔e7 34 ♔e3 ♔e6 35 ♔d4! intending b3, a4 winning (Seirawan).

28...♗e6 29 ♖d4 ♗xd5 30 ♖xd5 ♔e7 31 ♖b5 ♔e6 32 ♖b7 ♖c5?

Better was 32...a6 33 ♔d2 c3+! 34 bxc3 ♖c5= (Seirawan).

33 ♖xa7 g5 34 ♖a8 gxh4 35 ♖e8+ ♔d7 36 ♖e4 c3 37 ♖xh4?

Again White is winning with 37 b4! ♖g5 38 ♖xh4 ♖xg2 39 ♔b1! because of the connected passed pawns (Seirawan).

37...cxb2+ 38 ♔xb2

And after a few more missed opportunities for White, the game was drawn in 63 moves.

3: The Richter-Rauzer Variation

The Richter-Rauzer could also be called the "Anti-Dragon Variation". The intention of this system is immediately to put pressure on Black's centre. It is characterized by the move 6 ♗g5.

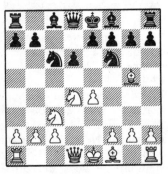

In this way White effectively prevents Black from playing the Dragon variation since, if now Black tries 6...g6, White can capture on f6 and damage Black's pawn structure. With ♗g5 White indirectly pins the black knight on f6 and will always be threatening to capture it, diverting either the black queen or the black bishop on e7. Alternatively, Black may recapture with the pawn on g7 leaving him with doubled pawns on f6 and f7. The resulting "house" around the black king (pawns on f7, f6, e6, d6)

may be strong or weak, depending on the position. Usually this house is precarious in the middle game and safe in the ending. The structure is illustrated below.

Black must be cautious about the possibility of a white knight landing on the d5 square after which it cannot be captured with impunity. Obviously such a knight is a thorn in Black's side since it attacks many critical squares and its capture ...exd5, exd5 might open up an attack directly against his king.

In some rare cases Black may be able to liquidate his doubled f-pawns with f5 thereby liberating a bishop on g7. More frequently, Black will play ...e5, driving a white knight from d4, and then follow with ...f5 or ...d5.

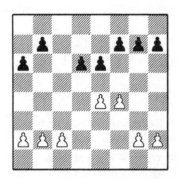

In this structure, if White is able to land a knight or bishop on f5 or d5 and Black is unable to oppose or trade off the piece, then Black can expect to suffer as a result of his weaknesses on the light squares.

One scheme often tried by White is to attack Black's "house" structure with f4-f5 and ♘c3-♘e2-f4. White endeavours to force Black to play ...e5 when the d5 square may again become a debilitating weakness. Game 2 is a great example of how Black may handle this kind of assault. It is noteworthy that as soon as Black is able to win the battle for the d5 square, he can follow with ...d5 (See Game 2). In this case, as is typical in the Rauzer, it is important for Black to follow quickly with ...d5, when the latent power of the bishops becomes apparent.

The typical Richter-Rauzer will develop with Black having pawns on d6, e6 and f7, while White will step up the pressure by forming a duo of pawns on f4 and e4.

White's duo will always be threatening e5 or f5. It is Black's continual responsibility in the Richter-Rauzer Variation to be able to deal with one or other of these pawn advances. Black will usually also place a pawn on a6, both to prevent ♘b5 and to threaten ...b5, advancing his attack on the queenside. If White's e4-e5 comes at any time in the first 15 moves or so and Black is unable to find a reasonable central move with his ♘f6 (e.g., ...♘d5, ...♘d7 or ...♘e4) without being encumbered with some long term weakness, king-safety or developmental problem, then this is evidence that Black has mishandled the opening.

Another possibility, which you will see in several games (Games 7, 10, and 11 particularly illustrate these ideas) is a willingness by Black to sacrifice his d-pawn in order to obtain long-term compensation in terms of an *initiative and control of the dark squares*. Such variations arise when White plays ♗xf6 and Black elects to recapture with his bishop on e7, thereby leaving Black's d-pawn without adequate defence. The Black player who sacrifices his d-pawn in this way must play in the spirit of the position: open lines, control the dark squares, develop quickly and *attack*.

RAUZER MASTERY
LESSON 1

Classic Sicilian Methods

■ **Early liquidations tend to ease Black's defensive task**

■ **When White and Black castle on opposite wings (which is typical in the Richter-Rauzer), both sides are compelled to attack**

■ **Black's natural play always begins on the half-open c-file**

■ **Structural defects can become decisive factors in the endgame**

Rauzer (Game 1)
P. Enders-V.Kramnik
Germany 1995

As this book goes to press, the chessworld has seen Vladimir Kramnik win a world title match against Garry Kasparov, ending the Champion's reign of 15 years.

One opening system which has served Kramnik extremely well is the Black side of the Richter-Rauzer variation of the Sicilian Defence.

Here is a typical example which illustrates the great confidence he has in his technical skills—even when holding only the smallest of positional advantages.

1 e4 c5 2 ♘f3 ♘c6 3 d4 cxd4 4 ♘xd4 ♘f6 5 ♘c3 d6 6 ♗g5 e6 7 ♕d2 ♗e7

A solid move. Other tries here are 7...♘xd4 8 ♕xd4 ♗d7 or 7...h6 8 ♗xf6 gxf6.

8 0-0-0 ♘xd4 9 ♕xd4 0-0 10 e5

Quite playable also is 10 f3, but 10 ♘b5? would be bad in view of 10...a6 11 ♘xd6 ♗xd6 12 ♕xd6 (12 ♗xf6? ♗f4+ would cost White a piece) 12...♕xd6 13 ♖xd6 ♘xe4 and Black wins the exchange.

10...dxe5 11 ♕xe5 ♗d7 12 ♗e2

After 12 ♕g3 ♘h5 13 ♗xe7 ♕xe7 (but not 13...♘xg3? 14 ♗xd8 ♘xh1 15 ♗e7 ♗c6 16 ♗xf8 ♔xf8 17 f3! when White is winning) 14 ♕e5 White is slightly better.

12...♖c8 13 ♗e3 ♗b4 14 ♗d4

White couldn't afford the terrible weakening of the queenside resulting from 14 ♗xa7 ♗xc3 15 bxc3.

14...♗c6 15 ♗f3

Now if 15 ♗xa7 ♗xc3 16 ♕xc3 (here 16 bxc3 would be met by 16...♗d5 threatening 17...♕a5 with an attack) 16...♗xg2 17 ♖xd8 ♖xc3 18 ♖xf8+ ♔xf8 19 bxc3 ♗xh1 when the bishop-pair would have made up for White's broken pawns.

15...♕a5!?

16 ♗xc6 ♖xc6 17 a3 ♕xe5 18 ♗xe5 ♗xc3 19 ♗xc3 ♖fc8 20 ♖d3

Kramnik is confident that his long-term positional pressure on the half-open c-file (which is a characteristic, fundamental feature of the Sicilian Defence in all its variations!) will ultimately lead to victory. His patience and quiet determination in this regard is most remarkable.

20...♘d5 21 ♔d2 ♔f8 22 ♖e1 ♖c4 23 f3 ♘xc3! 24 bxc3

24...♔e7

White's weak doubled pawn on c3 will require constant protection. Black's plan will be to advance pawns on the kingside so as to create weaknesses there, too. He will improve the position of his king in preparation for a final infiltration.

25 ♖b1 b6 26 ♖b4 g5 27 ♖xc4 ♖xc4 28 ♖d4 ♖c5 29 ♖a4 ♖c7 30 ♔d3

Naturally Black does not want to change the disposition of the pawns, as White's structure is inherently weak.

30...f5 31 h4 ♔f6 32 ♖d4 gxh4 33 ♖xh4 ♔g5 34 ♖d4 e5 35 ♖d8 ♔f4

And now Black begins the final infiltration with his king.

36 ♖g8 h5 37 ♔e2

On 37 ♖h8 comes 37...e4+ 38 fxe4 fxe4+ 39 ♔d4 ♖d7+ 40 ♔c4 e3 41 ♖e8 ♖d2 42 g3+ ♔f3 winning.

37...h4

The simplest move of course was 37...♖xc3.

38 ♖h8 ♖xc3 39 ♖xh4+ ♔g5 40 ♖h7 ♖xa3

Finally Black wins a pawn while retaining his positional superiority.

41 ♖g7+ ♔f6 42 ♖b7 f4

Fixing the weakness at g2 and creating the possibility of ...e4 and ...♔e5.

43 ♖b8 ♖c3 44 ♔d2 ♖c7 45 ♖f8+ ♖f7 46 ♖h8 ♖g7 47 ♖h2

White's rook is forced into a passive position.

47...e4!

Opening the way for the black king to enter into White's position.

48 fxe4 ♔e5 49 ♔c3 ♔xe4 50 ♔b2 ♖g3

Simpler was 50...♖g4 defending his f4-pawn.

51 ♔c1 ♔e3 52 ♔b2 ♖g4

But not 52...♔f2? 53 ♖h4 when White still has some play.

0-1

RAUZER MASTERY LESSON 2

Classic Rauzer Methods

■ When Black's f-pawns become doubled by ♗xf6, gxf6, the activity of his bishops becomes critical

■ If White can play f5 and Black responds with ...e5, then the struggle over the d5 square becomes critical

■ When (if) Black's bishops spring to life after a sound ...d5 he will most likely have the advantage

Rauzer (Game 2)
C.Vasiescu-N.Andrescu
Bucharest 1999

1 e4 c5 2 ♘f3 d6 3 d4 cxd4 4 ♘xd4 ♘f6 5 ♘c3 a6

This game starts out as a Najdorf Variation, but transposes into a type of "Rauzer Attack".

6 ♗g5 e6 7 ♕d3 ♘c6 8 0-0-0

This move introduces threats such as 9 ♘xc6 bxc6 10 e5 h6 11 ♗h4 g5 12 ♗g3 ♘d5 13 ♘e4 dxe5 14 ♗xe6 ♖g8 15 ♘f6+ ♔e7 16 ♕a3+ c5 17 ♕xc5+ ♕d6 18 ♕xd6 mate!

8...♕c7 9 f4 ♗d7 10 ♗xf6 gxf6

White breaks up Black's kingside pawn structure, but also parts with his bishop-pair.

11 ♔b1 0-0-0 12 ♗e2 h5

Avoiding the type of positional bind which can arise after White's

♗h5 and hoping for a future ...h4-h5 when he may find a way to attack the g2 and f4 pawns.

13 g3 ♔b8 14 ♘xc6+ ♕xc6

An awkward way to recapture, but it does not end up hurting Black.

15 ♗f3 ♕b6 16 ♘e2 ♗e7 17 ♘d4 ♖c8

Black's game looks pretty comfortable thanks to several exchanges, his two bishops and the fact that he has no major weaknesses.

18 ♖he1 ♖c7 19 f5 e5

A typical reaction when White attempts to exploit Black's doubled pawns. The battle now shifts to control of the d5 square.

20 ♘e2 ♖hc8 21 ♗xh5?!

Safer was 21 ♖c1 (21 ♖d2 ♕f2) although Black would maintain the initiative by 21...♗e8 with the idea of 22...♕f2.

21...♖xc2 22 ♕xc2 ♖xc2 23 ♔xc2 d5!

Opening the diagonal for his dark-squared bishop. Black now develops an attack with his queen and bishop-pair.

24 ♘c3

After 24 ♖xd5 would come 24...♗c6 and on 24 exd5 ♗xf5+.

24...♗b4

Immediately putting the newly-liberated black bishop to work. Now 25 ♘xd5 ♕c5+ 26 ♘c3 ♗a4+ loses material.

25 ♖xd5

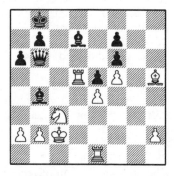

25...♗xc3

Giving White the choice of going for a walk with his king or allowing the break-up of his pawn formation.

26 ♔xc3 ♗c6

Also good was 26 ♗xf5 when 27 exf5 is met by 27...♕c6+ and 27 ♗xf7 by 27...♕c7+ 28 ♔d3 ♕xf7 winning.

27 ♖dd1

After 27 ♖d2 or ♖d3 27...♕a5+ was too strong.

27...♕c7

Also possible was 27...♕a5+.

28 ♔b3 ♕a5

Now on 29 ♗xf7 comes 29...♗a4+ 30 ♔c4 ♗xd1 31 ♖xd1 ♕c7+ 32 ♔d3 ♕xf7 winning.

29 ♔c2 ♕xa2

Threatening 30...♗a4+

30 ♖d8+ ♔c7 31 ♖d3 ♗a4+ 32 ♔c1 ♕a1+ 33 ♔d2 ♕xb2+ 34 ♔e3 ♕xh2 35 ♖c1+ ♗c6 36 ♗f3

On 36 g4 comes 36 ♕f4+.

36...♕h6+ 0-1

RAUZER MASTERY LESSON 3

Sharp Rauzer Methods

■ In some very specific Sicilian Variations (in the Rauzer and Najdorf) Black may be able to play an early ...h6 followed by ...g5

■ The sequence in this game with 9...h6 and 10...g5, coupled with 8...♗d7, is one such variation

■ In this instance control of the e5 square becomes critical for Black

■ Black's central and dark-squared control emanating from e5 can develop into a decisive positional bind

■ Black's doubled, isolated pawns on e6 and e5 can be very strong in certain Sicilian positions because of the number of central squares they control

---

Rauzer (Game 3)
P.Wells-Z.Kozul
Bled 1995

1 e4 c5 2 ♘f3 ♘c6 3 d4 cxd4 4 ♘xd4 ♘f6 5 ♘c3 d6 6 ♗g5 e6 7 ♕d2 a6 8 0-0-0 ♗d7 9 f4 h6 10 ♗h4 g5!?

A sharp move, blowing away White's central duo and leaving the e4 pawn isolated—after which

Black acquires the e5 square for his knight. Kozul is a Richter Rauzer specialist!

11 fxg5 ♘g4 12 ♘xc6

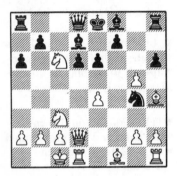

12...♗xc6 13 ♗e2 ♘e5 14 g3 ♘g6 15 ♖df1 ♕a5 16 ♗h5

In order to retain the pawn, White has accepted an awkward position.

16...♗e7 17 ♗xg6 fxg6 18 ♕d4

Of course 18 gxh6? g5 wins for Black.

18...♕e5 19 ♕xe5 dxe5

White is still a pawn up but his bishop is threatened by ...hxg5.

20 g4 b5

The white knight is very weak in this type of position, since it can be attacked and has no forward moves.

21 ♖f2 b4 22 ♘d1 h5!

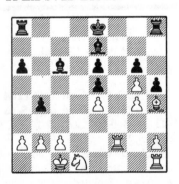

23 ♗g3

On 23 h3? hxg4 24 hxg4 ♖xh4 25 ♖xh4 ♗xg5+ wins a piece.

23...♗xg5+ 24 ♔b1 hxg4 25 ♗xe5 ♖h7

Black has re-established material equality and stands better due to his pair of bishops, the constellation on the h-file and the g4-pawn.

26 ♗d6?

White should defend the e4 pawn by ♖e2.

26...0-0-0 27 ♗xb4 g3!

White, probably in time pressure, didn't see this move after which Black gets an advanced passed pawn.

28 ♖e2 ♗f4 29 h3 ♖xh3

The h1-rook has to defend the knight.

30 ♖g1 ♖h2 31 ♘c3 ♖xe2 32 ♘xe2 ♗e3!

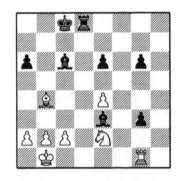

Controlling the queening square. The g3 pawn is taboo because on 33 ♖xg3 follows 33...♖d1+ and mate next move. Also, on 33 ♖e1 comes 33...g2, and the threat ...♖h8-♖h1 decides the game.

0-1

RAUZER MASTERY LESSON 4

Sharp Rauzer Struggles Unusual Methods

■ In Sicilians, the exchanges which follow ...e5, ♘f5, - ♗xf5, exf5 - can lead to very double-edged positions

■ In such instances Black will be especially weak on the light squares but strong on the dark squares

■ White's kingside pawn storm will tend to be slowed down in such variations

■ It is important that Black is active through the centre with his knights

■ Black must be cautious that the d5 square does not become too potent for White as a springboard to attack

■ Sometimes Black can shield his backward d-pawn with ...♘d4, especially if it is difficult to evict that knight by c2-c3

■ It is rare that two knights will outdo two bishops in attack if the knights are not centrally posted; but if the knights are able to penetrate deeply enough into the opposing camp unusual combinations may follow

■ An unusual, and surprising exchange sacrifice, perhaps for decoy effect, may be part and parcel of such a combination

Rauzer (Game 4)
R.Ziatdinov-D.Gurevich
Berne 1995

1 e4 c5 2 ♘f3 d6 3 d4 cxd4 4 ♘xd4 ♘f6 5 ♘c3 ♘c6 6 ♗g5 e6 7 ♕d2 ♗e7 8 0-0-0 0-0 9 f4 h6

The usual line is 9...♘xd4 10 ♕xd4 ♕a5 11 ♗c4 ♗d7 12 e5 dxe5 13 fxe5 ♗c6 etc.

10 ♗h4 ♕b6 11 ♗f2?!

This bishop doesn't do anything on f2. Better is 11 ♘xc6 followed by 12 e5.

11...♕c7 12 ♗e2

If 12 ♘db5?! ♕a5 is good for Black.

12...e5 13 ♘f5 ♗xf5 14 exf5 d5!

Black has achieved a very comfortable position. If now 15 ♘xd5 then 15...♘xd5 16 ♕xd5 exf4. Still, this was better than the continuation chosen by White in the game.

15 fxe5 ♕xe5 16 ♗g3 ♕xf5 17 ♘xd5 ♘e4

Black seizes the initiative.

18 ♘xe7+ ♘xe7 19 ♕d7 ♕g5+ 20 ♔b1 ♘f5

Strangely, even though the black knights are rather precariously placed, they are more effective than White's bishops.

21 ♗c7
If 21 ♕xb7 then 21...♘xg3 22 hxg3 ♘c3+ 23 bxc3 ♖ab8 winning.
21...♘e3 22 ♖de1 ♖ac8
Hitting the bishop which covers the c2-pawn. After 22...♘xg2? 23 ♖dg1 would pin the knight, while on 22...♕xg2? 23 ♗d3 White's position would spring to life. Black, threatening to win with 23...♕c5, now has a strategically won game.
23 ♗f3

23...♖xc7!
A very unusual combination which sets the stage for a decisive coordination of forces.
24 ♕xc7 ♘d2+ 25 ♔c1
More natural looking was 25 ♔a1, but then Black has 25...♕a5!! 26 ♕c3 (26 ♕xa5 ♘xc2 mate) 26...♕xc3 27 bxc3 ♘xc2+ 28 ♔b2 ♘xe1 29 ♖xe1 ♘xf3 30 gxf3 with a won ending.
25...♘ec4 26 ♖d1
If 26 ♔d1, then 26...♘xf3 27 gxf3 ♕d2 mate.
26...♘b3+
Now if 27 ♔b1, then 27...♕c1+! 28 ♖xc1 ♘cd2 mate.
0-1

**RAUZER MASTERY
LESSON 5**

Liquidation - Central Control - Attack

■ **When Black can successfully castle, achieving king safety coupled with liquidations, he is generally in good shape in the Rauzer**

■ **Once the above is achieved, Black should strive for attack on the white king**

■ **An attack will often stem from the centre to the white king**

Rauzer (Game 5)
J.Fernandes-E.Limp
Rio de Janeiro, 1999

1 e4 c5 2 ♘f3 ♘c6 3 d4 cxd4 4 ♘xd4 ♘f6 5 ♘c3 d6 6 ♗g5 e6 7 ♕d2 ♗e7 8 0-0-0 ♘xd4 9 ♕xd4 0-0 10 f4 ♕a5
Other typical moves here are 10...a6 and 10...h6.
11 ♔b1
White refrains from the main variation starting with 11 ♗c4; other alternatives are 11 ♗b5 and 11 e5.
11...♖d8 12 ♗e2 ♗d7 13 e5 dxe5 14 fxe5 ♗c6 15 ♕f4 ♘d5 16 ♘xd5 ♗xg5 17 ♕xg5 ♗xd5
The comparison between this position and one which occurred in a recent game of mine (see Game 11 below) is especially noteworthy.
18 a3 ♗e4

Also interesting is 18...b5.

19 ♕f4

Hoping to obtain an attack for a pawn.

19...♗xg2 20 ♖hg1 ♖xd1+ 21 ♗xd1 ♗c6 22 ♗e2

White should try 22 ♕g5 g6 23 h4 and hope for the best.

22...g6 23 h4 ♕c5 24 ♖g3 ♖d8 25 h5 ♖d4 26 ♕f6

Better was 26 ♕g5, controlling the d2 square.

26...♖d2 27 ♗d3

27...♗d5

Black threatens mate. Instead of the text move, 27...♗b5?? would have allowed 28 ♕d8+ ♔g7 29 ♕f6+ etc. with a perpetual check.

28 ♔c1

On 28 b3 Black has 18...♕c3 still threatening mate.

28...♖f2 29 ♕h4

After 29 ♕d8+ ♔g7 30 h6+ ♔xh6 31 ♖h3+ ♔g7 White just loses a second pawn.

29...♗b3 30 hxg6

On 30 c3 Black would also win a second pawn by 30...♕xe5, threatening 31...♕e1 mate.

30...♖xc2+

If 31 ♔d1 then 31...♖h2+ 32 ♔e1 ♕c1 is mate.

0-1

**RAUZER MASTERY
LESSON 6**

**Sharp Rauzer Struggles -
Unusual Methods**

■ In opposite wing attacks not all pawn sacrifices will be justified

■ The key is open lines (files and diagonals) to the opposing king

■ When White must respond to ...b4 with ♘a4, this knight may be forced permanently offside

■ Black should always concentrate on control of the centre

■ Via the centre, Black can more easily defend his own king while remaining within striking distance of the white king

Rauzer (Game 6)
A.Kornev-V.Belikov
Moscow 1995

1 e4 c5 2 ♘f3 ♘c6 3 d4 cxd4 4 ♘xd4 ♘f6 5 ♘c3 d6 6 ♗g5 ♕b6

Black gains a tempo which he will later have to return because his queen is not well placed.

7 ♘b3 e6 8 ♕d2 ♗e7 9 0-0-0 0-0 10 f3 ♖d8 11 ♔b1

An interesting alternative is 11 ♘b5, threatening 12 ♗e3.

11...♕c7

11...d5 is also possible.

12 h4 a6 13 h5

With the idea of h6, weakening the dark squares around the black king.

13...h6 14 ♗h4 b5 15 g4 ♘e5 16 ♕f2 b4 17 ♘a4 ♖b8

The typical Sicilian race on opposite wings. Note that by quite simple and sound means Black obtains a good game while White's offside knight is trapped on a4.

18 ♗g3

If 18 g5 then 18...hxg5 19 ♗xg5 ♕c6 wins a piece. But now 18...♕c6 can be answered with ♘ac5.

18...♗b7 19 g5

White sacrifices a pawn in the hope of kingside counterplay.

19...hxg5 20 ♘d4

20...g4!

Black immediately puts the pawn to work and brings about the disintegration of White's centre.

21 h6 g6 22 h7+ ♔h8

But not 22...♘xh7 23 ♕h2.

23 ♗d3 gxf3 24 ♘xf3 ♘xe4 25 ♗xe4 ♗xe4 26 ♘xe5 dxe5

Black now has a completely won game. Not only is he two pawns up,

but White's attack is stalled: his knight remains trapped on a4, and 27 ♕xf7 is met by 27...♕xc2+ followed by mate.

27 ♖he1 ♖xd1+ 28 ♖xd1 f6 29 ♕e2 ♖d8 30 ♖e1 ♗f5

To cap it all Black has a tremendous defensive quartet in front of his king.

31 b3 ♕d6 32 ♖c1 ♕c6 33 ♘b2 ♗c5

Black prepares for the final assault on the dark squares leading to the enemy king.

34 ♗h4 g5 35 ♗g3 ♗d4 36 ♘c4 ♕e4 37 ♕h5 ♗xh7 38 ♕f7 ♕g6 39 ♕e7

On 39 ♕xe6 very strong is 39 ♗c5 taking away the d6 square from the black knight and threatening 40...♕xc2+! 41 ♖xc2 ♖d1+ 42 ♔b2 ♗d4+ 43 ♖c3 ♖b1 mate (or 43 ♗xc3 mate).

39...♖e8 40 ♕d7 ♖f8 0-1

White resigns because he has no play. On 41 ♕xe6 Black could, for example, continue with simply 41...e4 followed by rolling up his kingside pawns.

RAUZER MASTERY
LESSON 7

**Pawn Sacrifice for the
Two Bishops and
Dark-squared Control**

■ In some Sicilian lines Black
can comfortably sacrifice a
pawn for good development,
two bishops and control of the
dark squares

■ Pawn advances on the
queenside will commonly lead
to the exposure of the white
king

■ Exchanges which lead to
open lines against the white
king need not be avoided

Rauzer (Game 7)
V.Jansa-V.Babula
Rishon 1995

1 e4 c5 2 ♘c3 ♘c6 3 ♘ge2 d6 4
d4 cxd4 5 ♘xd4 ♘f6 6 ♗g5 e6 7
♕d2 ♗e7 8 0-0-0 0-0 9 ♘b3
On 9 ♘db5, good for Black is 9
♕e5 10 ♗xf6 ♗xf6 11 ♘xd6 ♖d8.
9...♕b6
Two interesting alternatives are
9...a5 and 9...d5.
10 f3 a6 11 ♗xf6!? ♗xf6
Black sacrifices a pawn to obtain
a tremendous dark-squared bishop
and the possibility of a quick
counterattack on the queenside.
**12 ♕xd6 ♖d8 13 ♕c5 ♖xd1+ 14
♔xd1**

The recapture 14 ♘xd1 would
have been too passive.
14...♕c7

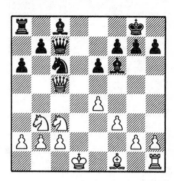

Black's control of the dark
squares and superior mobility, in
conjunction with White's rather
exposed king, suggests sufficient
compensation for a pawn.
15 ♕e3
Preventing Black from playing
...♕f4.
15...b5 16 f4 b4
This move, introducing Black's
usual Sicilian queenside counterplay, is even more effective than
usual because the white king is also
a target.
17 ♘a4 e5!
Now that White can no longer
jump to d5, Black fights for control
of the central dark squares.
**18 f5 ♘d4 19 ♗d3 ♗d7 20 ♘ac5
♗b5**
Black can play this move because
21 ♗xb5? axb5 results in the loss of
the a2 pawn.
21 ♕d2 ♘c6!
Black defends b4 and is ready to
create problems for White with
22...♗e7 hitting the ♘c5.
22 ♔c1 ♗e7 23 h4 ♕a7

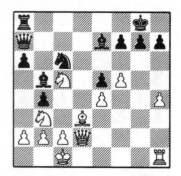

Finally, Black exploits the position of the ♘c5. If now 24 ♕f2 Black can counter with ...♘d4 or ...♖c8.

24 ♗xb5 axb5 25 ♘d3

White would have more chances with 25 ♕d5. One continuation might be 25 ♕d5 ♘d4 26 ♘xd4 exd4 (26...♗xc5 27 ♘c6 ♕xa2 28 ♕xa2 ♖xa2 29 ♔b1 and White is better) 27 ♘d3 and White seems okay.

25...♕xa2

Black obviously threatens mate.

26 ♔d1 ♖d8

Black targets the white king directly.

27 ♔e2 ♘d4+ 28 ♘xd4 ♖xd4

The incursion of this rook into White's camp spells doom.

29 ♕e3 ♕c4 30 ♔f3 ♕xc2 31 ♘xe5 ♖d2

More effective would have been 31...♗c5 with the devastating threat of ...♖d2. On 32 ♕a7 ♕b3+! would win for Black.

32 ♖a1 f6 33 ♖a8+ ♗f8 34 ♕b6 ♕b3+ 35 ♔g4 ♖xg2+ 36 ♔h5 ♕d1+

Mate follows.

0-1

**RAUZER MASTERY
LESSON 8**

Liquidation - Central Control - Attack

■ **When Black can successfully castle, achieving king safety coupled with liquidation, he is generally in good shape**

■ **Once the above is achieved, Black should strive for an attack on the white king**

■ **Attack will often stem from the centre to the white king**

■ **Aggressive pawn advances coupled with gain of space may facilitate Black's play**

Rauzer (Game 8)
N.Kalesis-V.Kotronias
Greece 1995

1 e4 c5 2 ♘f3 ♘c6 3 d4 cxd4 4 ♘xd4 ♘f6 5 ♘c3 d6 6 ♗g5 e6 7 ♕d2 ♗e7 8 0-0-0 0-0 9 ♘b3 ♕b6 10 ♗e3

This seems a more promising continuation than going after Black's d-pawn, as seen in the previous game. The bishop gets out of the path of the g2 pawn which can now march to g5. 10 ♗e3 also creates possibilities on the queenside and can even slow down Black's play on that wing. The position has now essentially transposed into a type of "English Attack" against the Scheveningen which we saw earlier.

10...♕c7 11 f4 a6

Although, strictly speaking, this move weakens the queenside, it is Black's main method of initiating counterplay.

12 ♗d3 b5 13 h3 ♘d7 14 ♕f2

White prevents ...♘b6.

14...♘b4 15 ♔b1 ♗b7 16 g4 ♘xd3

The gain of the bishop-pair is usually to Black's advantage.

17 cxd3 b4 18 ♘a4 d5 19 ♘b6?

Necessary was 19 ♘ac5. Instead of his next move, Black should play 19...dxe4 with excellent compensation for the exchange after 20 ♘xa8 ♖xa8 etc.

19...♖ad8? 20 ♖c1 ♕b8 21 ♘xd7 ♖xd7 22 ♘c5 ♖dd8 23 ♘xb7 ♕xb7 24 e5 d4

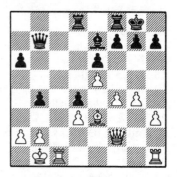

An excellent idea since on 25 ♗xd4 ♕d5 is very strong for Black.

25 ♗d2 b3 26 a3 ♕d5 27 ♖he1 ♖c8

It is clear that Black now has the more aggressive position with more space.

28 f5

White hopes to create counterplay by f6.

28...♖xc1+ 29 ♗xc1 ♖c8 30 f6 ♗f8 31 ♖e4 ♕c6! 32 ♕d2 g6

Black refrains from defending d4 since 32...♖xd4 will allow an incursion by the black queen.

33 ♖xd4 ♕f3

Here, one continuation might be 34 ♕h2 ♖c2 35 ♕f4 ♕d1, threatening ...♖xb2+ with mate to follow.

34 ♕e3 ♕g2 35 ♕d2 ♕xh3 36 ♕d1 ♕h2 37 ♗f4 ♕f2 38 ♖a4 ♖c2 39 ♗c1

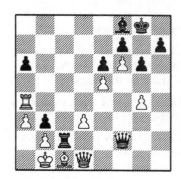

39...h5!

Excellent because it

(1) creates some room for the Black king on h7;

(2) threatens ...♗h6 which is otherwise answered by ♖xa6;

(3) creates a passed pawn.

40 gxh5 ♗h6!

A nice combination since if If 41 ♗xh6 ♖xb2+ 42 ♔c1 ♖b1+! 43 ♔xb1 ♕a2+ 44 ♔c1 b2+ 45 ♔d2 b1=♕+ winning.

41 ♖c4 ♗xc1 42 ♖xc2 bxc2+ 43 ♕xc2 ♕xc2+ 44 ♔xc2 ♗xb2!

The simplest! After 45 ♔xb2 gxh5 the h-pawn queens.

0-1

RAUZER MASTERY LESSON 9

Liquidation - Central Control - Attack

■ Bear in mind that the "pawn island theory" tends to favour Black in the Sicilian

■ When Black can successfully castle achieving king safety coupled with liquidation, he is generally in good shape

■ Once the above is achieved, Black should strive for an attack on the white king

■ Attack will often stem from the centre to the white king

■ Aggressive pawn advances coupled with gain of space may facilitate Black's play

Rauzer (Game 9)
T.Luther-Z.Hraček
Altensteig 1995

1 e4 c5 2 ♘f3 ♘c6 3 d4 cxd4 4 ♘xd4 ♘f6 5 ♘c3 d6 6 ♗g5 e6 7 ♕d2 ♗e7 8 0-0-0 0-0 9 h4

Quite an aggressive gesture.

9...♘xd4 10 ♕xd4 ♕a5

Black could play ...a6 and ...b5 or ...a6 and ...♕c7.

11 ♕d2 ♖d8 12 ♔b1 ♕c7

Black probably wanted to avoid 12...a6 13 ♘d5 ♕xd2 14 ♘xe7+ ♔f8 15 ♖xd2 ♔xe7 16 h5 h6 17 ♗h4 when White has the advantage of the two bishops.

13 f4 a6

After 13...h6 14 ♗d3 hxg5 15 hxg5 ♘d7 16 g3, White, due to the threat of 17 ♕h2, would have a very dangerous attack.

14 ♗d3 b5 15 a3?!

Weakeing the queenside. Better is 15 h5, and if 15...b4 then 16 ♘e2.

15...♖b8 16 e5 dxe5 17 fxe5 ♘d5

But not 17...♕xe5? 18 ♗f4.

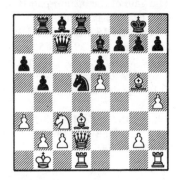

18 ♘xd5

On 18 ♘e4 strong was 18...b4 19 a4 ♘c3+.

18...♖xd5 19 ♕f4 b4

19...♖xe5? 20 ♗xe7 was bad, and 19 ♗xg5 20 hxg5 equally so.

20 a4 ♗b7 21 ♗xe7 ♕xe7 22 ♗e4 ♖dd8 23 b3 a5 24 ♖hf1 ♗xe4 25 ♕xe4 ♖d7 26 ♕c6 ♖bd8

26...♖xd1+ 27 ♖xd1 ♕xh4 28 ♕c7 would have given White compensation for the pawn.

27 ♔c1!? ♖c7 28 ♖xd8+ ♕xd8 29 ♕f3 h6 30 ♖d1?! ♕xh4 31 ♕a8+ ♔h7 32 ♕xa5 ♖c3 33 ♕b5 ♕f2 34 ♖d2 ♕f4 35 a5?

Necessary was 35 ♕e2 ♖e3 36 ♕f2, but now 36...♕xe5 gives Black the advantage.

35...♖e3 36 ♔b2 ♖xe5 37 ♕d3+ f5 38 a6 ♖d5 0-1

White must resign because, after, for example, 39 a7 ♕e5+ 40 ♔b1 ♖xd3 41 ♖xd3 ♕a5, Black wins.

**RAUZER MASTERY
LESSON 10**

**The Simagin Variation
and its Endings**

■ **Black can play the Simagin
Variation, (...a6, ♗e7, ♗d7,
...b5) and gambit his d-pawn
for smooth development and
counterplay**

■ **Sometimes Black can
capture on c3 and trade queens
to reach an equal ending**

■ **Black should never lose
sight of his strategic objectives
on the half-open c-file**

Rauzer (Game 10)
J.Barrios-D.Kopec
North Atlantic Correspondence
Team Tournament,
(USA vs. Spain), 1995-1997

The following game illustrates
one of my favourite systems in the
Richter Rauzer, the Simagin Variation, which is characterized by
10...b5 11 ♗xf6 ♗xf6 12 ♕xd6
♖a7 etc.

**1 e4 c5 2 ♘f3 ♘c6 3 d4 cxd4 4
♘xd4 ♘f6 5 ♘c3 d6 6 ♗g5 e6 7
♕d2 ♗e7 8 0-0-0 a6 9 f4 ♗d7 10
♘f3 b5 11 ♗xf6 ♗xf6 12 ♕xd6**
The Simagin Variation, in which
Black sacrifices his d-pawn to keep
his pawn structure intact. It is one of
those systems which I call "so old
that it is new". It was popular in the

1960s before many of today's leading players were even born. The few
players who are aware of the
variation (from White's perspective)
are unlikely to be particularly well-
prepared for it.

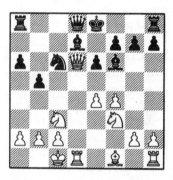

12...♖a7
The game J. Peters-Kopec, Brown
University Open, 1976, continued
12...b4 13 ♘a4 ♖a7 14 ♕c5 ♗e7 15
♕e3 ♕a5 16 b3 ♖b7 17 ♘d2 ♘b8!
(this "Rauzer knight move" has won
two games for me—see Kaplan-
Kopec, Game 11 below) 18 ♘c4
♕c7 19 e5 ♗xa4 20 bxa4 0-0 21 g4
♘d7 22 f5 ♖c8 23 a5 ♖b5 and
Black is better. Black can also play
12...♗e7 when a transposition after
13 ♕d2 ♖a7 14 e5 is possible, but
White may also try to improve with
13 ♕d3 etc.

13 e5 ♗e7 14 ♕d2 ♕a5
I had two previous over-the-board
games with this variation, one
against IM Craig Pritchett in Scotland in the late 1970s, and the other
against GM Michael Rohde in the
World Chess Festival Open in St.
John, New Brunswick, Canada, in
1988. In both games I failed to play
my principal idea which follows
here.

15 ♔b1 ♝b4 16 ♘g5

This is the idea. Black should trade on c3 because this inflicts significant damage on White's pawn structure. Black should certainly not wait for ♘ge4 after which White can consolidate.

16...♝xc3 17 bxc3

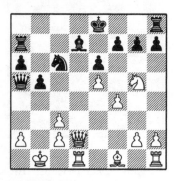

17...♜c7!

White's c-pawns will always be a target. I have played the text move many times—with considerable success.

18 ♕d6 ♘e7! 19 ♕b4 ♕xb4+ 20 cxb4 ♝c6 21 ♖g1 ♘d5 22 ♖d4 ♘c3+ 23 ♔b2 h6 24 ♘f3 ♝d5 25 ♝d3 ♔e7 26 ♖a1 ♖hc8 27 ♘e1 f5

I offered a draw here to secure a Correspondence IM Norm, but Black may well be better. ½-½

Rauzer (Game 11)
R.Fischer-B.Spassky
World Championship, Reykjavik, 1972

1 e4 c5 2 ♘f3 ♘c6 3 d4 cxd4 4 ♘xd4 ♘f6 5 ♘c3 d6 6 ♝g5 e6 7 ♕d2 a6 8 0-0-0 ♝d7 9 f4 ♝e7 10 ♝e2

Recently I was invited to a small tournament in New Hampshire where in the 4th Round I met GM Alexander Stripunsky. He claimed he did not know the position after ♝e2—and I had forgotten that this was the move played by Fischer in 1972 in the 20th game of his match against Spassky! In any case, although from White's point of view the move is both flexible and logical, preparing a kingside pawn storm with g4, it is also harmless for Black.

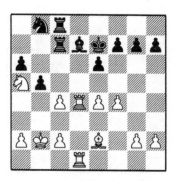

10...0-0

Stripunsky-Kopec, Petersborough, New Hampshire, continued 10...♘xd4 11 ♕xd4 ♕a5 12 e5 dxe5 13 fxe5 ♗c6 (possibly even better is 13...0-0-0!) 14 ♕f4 ♘d5 15 ♘xd5 ♗xg5 16 ♕xg5 ♗xd5 17 ♕xg7 0-0-0 which was just short of equality after 18 a3 ♖hg8 19 ♕xf7 etc. Sometimes I wonder if I wasn't "smarter" 25 years ago. In a key game against Julio Kaplan, former World Junior Champion, en route to winning one of my first Open tournaments, the Continental, New York 1975, I played **10...♖c8** with play continuing **11 ♘b3 b5 12 ♗xf6 ♗xf6 13 ♕xd6 ♗xc3 14 bxc3 ♕c7**

As I've already mentioned previously, I don't believe that Black has anything to fear in ensuing endings.

15 ♔b2 ♕xd6 16 ♖xd6 ♔e7 17 ♖hd1 ♘b8!

The first time that I played this redeployment of the knight which leads to an ideal positioning on b6.

18 ♖6d4 ♖c7

By simple means Black defends his second rank and builds up pressure on the c-file.

19 ♘a5 ♖hc8 20 c4?!

20...e5! 21 fxe5 ♗e6 22 ♔a1 bxc4 23 ♖b1 ♘d7

Finally this knight begins its decisive re-entry into the game. White was now in serious time trouble.

24 ♖d6 ♘xe5 25 ♖xa6 ♖d7

For the time being the white knight has been salvaged—but not his position.

26 ♖e1 ♖d2 27 ♔b1 ♖c7 28 ♔c1 ♖d6!

Black hits upon an important theme: after the trade of rooks White's knight on a5 will be trapped. If White does not trade rooks Black can play ...♘d3+.

29 ♖xd6 ♔xd6 30 ♖d1+ ♔c5

And now it is apparent that the white knight on a5 is a "walk-off" for Black.

31 ♔b2 ♖a7 32 ♘b3+ cxb3 33 axb3 ♖d7 34 ♖xd7 ♗xd7 35 ♔c3 ♘c6 36 ♗c4 ♗e6 37 ♗xe6 fxe6

Black knows that two pawns should not be enough for a piece.

38 h3 ♘e5 39 b4+ ♔b5 40 ♔d4 ♘c6+

And White resigned.

0-1

Now we go back to the **Fischer-Spassky** game...

11 ♗f3

After the normal-looking 11 g4, Black could continue 11...♘xd4 12 ♕xd4 ♗c6 and is in good shape.

11...h6

12 h4!? is far too unclear and optimistic for a player of Fischer's precise and sober tastes.

12 ♗h4

12...♘xe4!

This little combination soon makes it clear that the game will end in a draw. So Fischer's 10th-12th moves fail to convince that White has an advantage.

13 ♗xe7 ♘xd2 14 ♗xd8 ♘xf3 15 ♘xf3 ♖fxd8 16 ♖xd6 ♔f8 17 ♖hd1 ♔e7 18 ♘a4 ♗e8 19 ♖xd8 ♖xd8 20 ♘c5 ♖b8 21 ♖d3 a5 22 ♖b3 b5 23 a3 a4 24 ♖c3 ♖d8

And the game ended in a **draw** in 54 moves.

RAUZER MASTERY LESSON 12

Secondary Variations by White

■ If White's play leaves Black with doubled f-pawns Black must counter on the queenside and centre

■ Black must concentrate on control of the dark squares

■ Black must be prepared to handle the attack on the central light squares initiated with f5

■ At the right time Black may counter with ...b5, ...b4 and/or ...e5

Rauzer (Game 12)
R.Fischer-B.Spassky
World Championship,
Reykjavik 1972

We give the following game as a typical dynamic struggle for the advantage between Black's pawn centre and two bishops and White's attempts to exploit the weaknesses in his opponent's position.

1 e4 c5 2 ♘f3 d6 3 ♘c3 ♘c6 4 d4 cxd4 5 ♘xd4 ♘f6 6 ♗g5 e6 7 ♕d2 a6 8 0-0-0 ♗d7 9 f4 ♗e7 10 ♘f3 b5 11 ♗xf6 gxf6 12 ♗d3 ♕a5

The other main continuation is to play 12 b4, and on 13 ♘e2 ♕b6 etc.

13 ♔b1 b4 14 ♘e2 ♕c5

Notice how Spassky recognizes the importance of keeping a grip on the dark squares while at the same time preparing to advance his queenside.

15 f5

This is the characteristic lever which attacks Black's centre.

15...a5 16 ♘f4 a4 17 ♖c1

White prepares to play c3 at an opportune moment.

17...♖b8 18 c3 b3 19 a3

The changes in the pawn structure have left Black with the more aggressive position (thanks to latent back rank threats) while White's position is sounder (two pawn islands, few weaknesses).

19...♘e5 20 ♖hf1 ♘c4 21 ♗xc4 ♕xc4

There follows a classic struggle of two knights against two bishops.

22 ♖ce1 ♔d8 23 ♔a1 ♖b5 24 ♘d4 ♖a5 25 ♘d3 ♔c7 26 ♘b4 h5 27 g3 ♖e5 28 ♘d3 ♖b8

Now on 29 ♘xe5 dxe5, 30 ♘ moves ♗c6, with ...♗xa3 often threatening, Black has a very dangerous initiative despite being the exchange down.

29 ♕e2 ♖a5 30 fxe6 fxe6 31 ♖f2 e5 32 ♘f5 ♗xf5 33 ♖xf5

Gradually, with this exchange, the tension is eased a little and White has better chances of surviving into an ending—but his back rank will still be a problem for a long time to come.

33...d5 34 exd5 ♕xd5 35 ♘b4 ♕d7 36 ♖xh5 ♗xb4 37 cxb4 ♖d5 38 ♖c1+ ♔b7 39 ♕e4 ♖c8 40 ♖b1 ♔b6

Black's activity just compensates for his pawn minus.

41 ♖h7 ♖d4 42 ♕g6 ♕c6 43 ♖f7 ♖d6 44 ♕h6 ♕f3 45 ♕h7 ♕c6 46 ♕h6 ♕f3 47 ♕h7 ♕c6 ½-½

4: The Characteristic Boleslavsky Structure

The Paulsen or Boleslavsky structure arises when Black plays an early ...e5 or, as mentioned earlier, it can be reached from a Scheveningen (or Najdorf) when Black plays ...e5, usually after an earlier ...e6. The Paulsen structures are distinct from the Najdorf in that in the Paulsen Black's queen's knight is ordinarily developed on c6 while in the Najdorf the queen's knight is developed on d7.

White usually follows with f4, establishing a duo.

Then Black may capture on f4 with ...exf4, followed by ♘e5.

The resulting structure is one where Black has an isolated d-pawn and White has an isolated e-pawn.

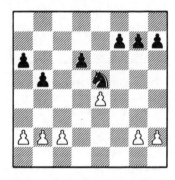

White retains the d5 square as an outpost, but it is noteworthy that here and in other continuations with the Boleslavsky/Paulsen formation, if for example after ♘d5 Black captures on d5 with a minor piece and White must recapture with exd5, the structure often turns decidedly in Black's favour.

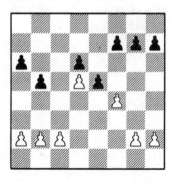

Descendent Structures from the Boleslavsky Sicilian favour Black, especially if Black can meet fxe5 with a piece capture on e5.

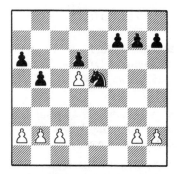

One of the main notions behind the Paulsen/Boleslasky system is that, throughout the middlegame, Black can live with his backward d-pawn, mainly because it is not easily assailable with minor pieces and he can defend this pawn as much as it is attacked. There is also a very dynamic quality to the system in that if Black is able to put pressure on White's e-pawn with ...♘f6, ...♗b7 and possibly ...♘c5, he also facilitates the powerful lever, ...d5.

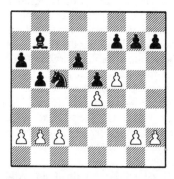

Black's queen's knight on b6 in Najdorf Systems supports ...d5 and also threatens to place itself on c4.

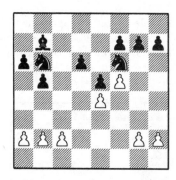

However, the worst Boleslavsky Sicilian forms occur when Black's knight gets driven from f6 and White has an effective kingside avalanche of pawns. In these cases Black has little or no pressure on White's e-pawn, and loses in the battle for control of the d5 square.

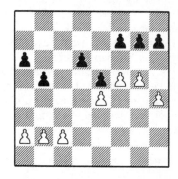

A. The Najdorf Variation

The Najdorf Variation is named after the late, famous Polish-Argentinian Grandmaster, Miguel Najdorf. However, the player who probably deserves the most credit for popularizing the Najdorf Variation is none other than Bobby Fischer. In his heyday in the 1950s and 60s an opponent could fully expect to see the Najdorf Variation from Fischer, but few people were ever able to get the upper hand in this variation against him. In time, Fischer's victories as Black in the Najdorf became classics of Sicilian history.

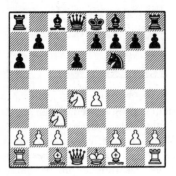

The Najdorf Variation is itself defined by the move 6...a6, when Black prepares an early ...b5 combined with ...♘bd7 and ...♗b7. In general, it is a very flexible and dynamic Sicilian system for Black. It is a more dynamic system than the Scheveningen because of the position of Black's knight on d7— which can now help to support ...d5 (after ...♘b6) or ...e5.

White has, over time, tried many alternatives against the Najdorf, including the aggressive, "Sozin" setup with ♗c4, the ♗g5 variation, ♗e2 (the Boleslavsky Variation), systems with h3, or f3 and g4. The system with ♗g5 seems to lead to the most complications (see Game 4) and there are sub-systems such as the Poisoned Pawn in which Black can initiate great complications.

Ironically, the single game which I might call the "The Perfect Sicilian" involves Bobby Fischer—but on the wrong side, as White against Tal!

NAJDORF MASTERY LESSON 1

"The Perfect Sicilian"

■ The Najdorf is based on the deployment ...d6, ...♘f6, ...e6 ...a6, ...b5, ...♘bd7, ...♗b7 and ...♗e7

■ After ...b5, ...b4 is usually a threat affecting White's defence of the centre

■ Sometimes Black may follow with ...♗c6, ...♕e7, ...♕b7 and ...d5

■ When Black achieves a sound ...d5 he may even have the advantage

Najdorf (Game 1)
R. Fischer-M. Tal
Candidates, Bled 1959

This game, played between Mikhail Tal and Bobby Fischer at the 1959 Candidates Tournament in Yugoslavia, can be viewed as a model for handling the Black side of the Najdorf Sicilian structure. It did not hurt Tal to know exactly what system he was likely to face from Fischer—namely the Sozin Variation which is spearheaded by ♗c4 and an attack by f4-f5 to maximise the activity of White's bishop.

1 e4 c5 2 ♘f3 d6 3 d4 cxd4 4 ♘xd4 ♘f6 5 ♘c3 a6 6 ♗c4 e6

In a later game at Sousse 1967, Fischer played 7 ♗e3 with the idea of ♕e2 and castling long.

7 ♗b3 ♗e7 8 f4 0-0 9 ♕f3 ♕c7 10 0-0 b5

Now on 11 e5 Black has 11...♗b7.

11 f5

Fischer plays the characteristic attacking move of the Sozin variation. Tal proceeds with his queenside and central pawn moves to force the white knights out of action and pressurise White's e-pawn.

11...b4 12 ♘a4 e5 13 ♘e2 ♗b7 14 ♘g3 ♘bd7

Black completes his development and has a simple plan to increase his pressure on the white e-pawn while preparing to enforce ...d5. Black will follow with ...♗c6 and ...♕b7 and there is little that White can do in response to this manoeuvre.

15 ♗e3 ♗c6 16 ♗f2 ♕b7 17 ♖fe1

17...d5

This move caps Black's strategy as White's centre collapses. It is the defining move for "The Perfect Sicilian".

18 exd5 ♘xd5

Black's threats on the a8-h1 diagonal are already deadly.

19 ♘e4 ♘f4 20 c4

20...g6!

The star move in this game in that Black enforces the e5-f5 duo. A wonderful lever.

21 fxg6 f5 22 g7 ♚xg7 23 ♕g3+ ♚h8 24 ♘ec5 ♘xc5 25 ♗xc5

Now Black could err with 25...♖g8? or 25...♗xg2? both of which could be met with 26 ♕xf4!! when White would turn the tables.

25...♗xc5+ 26 ♘xc5 ♕c7

Instead Black maintains his duo and his threats.

27 ♕e3 ♖ae8 28 ♖e2

There was no other way to meet Black's threat on g2.

28...♘xe2+ 29 ♕xe2 ♗xg2 30 ♘xa6 ♕a7+ 31 ♚xg2 ♖g8+ 32 ♚h3 ♕g7 0-1

White Resigned. A game which leaves a strong and lasting impression of how the Black side of the Najdorf Sicilian can and should be played.

NAJDORF MASTERY LESSON 2

Najdorf Theoretical Lines

■ The Najdorf is based on the deployment ...d6, ...♘f6, ...e6 ...a6, ...b5, ...♘bd7, ...♗b7 and ...♗e7

■ When White plays an early f4 coupled with 0-0 Black may choose this setup, "The Boleslavsky Wall"

■ The "Wall" is based on ...d6, ...e5, ...♘bd7, ...♕c7, ...♘f6, ♗b7, with a delayed kingside fianchetto to follow

■ It is important for Black always to be on the alert for f5

■ After ...b5, ...b4 is usually a threat affecting White's defence of the centre

■ Black often obtains counterplay with ...♘h5

■ The setup is rock-solid and Fischer won many games with it

Najdorf (Game 2)
R.Sanguinetti-R.Fischer
Portoroz Interzonal, 1958

When faced with 6 f4 against the Najdorf, Fischer would play the Boleslavsky/Paulsen setup with a delayed kingside fianchetto and ...♘bd7.

1 e4 c5 2 ♘f3 d6 3 d4 cxd4 4 ♘xd4 ♘f6 5 ♘c3 a6 6 f4 e5 7 ♘f3 ♕c7 8 ♗d3 ♘bd7 9 0-0 b5 10 ♕e1 ♗b7 11 ♘h4?

This turns out to be a loss of time. Better was 11 a3 and 12 ♔h1.

11...g6

This is a rock-solid setup which Fischer has used on many occasions.

12 ♘f3 ♗g7 13 ♕h4 0-0 14 fxe5 dxe5 15 ♗h6 ♘h5 16 ♗xg7 ♔xg7 17 ♖ad1 ♘f4

Tempting 18 ♘xe5? ♘xg2 with a big advantage for Black.

18 ♖f2 f6

Black already has a strategically won game because (1) White has no good levers; (2) White's e-pawn is weak; (3) Black's pieces are better positioned; (4) The ♘f4 is a thorn in White's position and (5) White has three pawn islands to Black's two.

19 ♖fd2 ♘c5 20 ♗f1?

A blunder which loses material.

20...b4 21 ♘d5 ♗xd5 22 exd5 ♘e4 23 ♕e1 ♘xd2 24 ♕xd2 ♘xd5

White could resign now.

25 c4 bxc3 White Resigns.

If 26 ♕xd5 ♕b6+ and then ...♖ad8.

**NAJDORF MASTERY
LESSON 3**

The "Theoretical Najdorf"

■ The Najdorf is based on the deployment ...d6, ...♘f6, ...e6 ...a6, ...b5, ...♘bd7, ...♗b7 and ...♗e7

■ After 0-0-0, ♕f3, and ♗d3, Black may delay ...0-0, finding some degree of safety for his king on the queenside

■ After Black castles long and White captures on g7 Black may not have sufficient compensation. Better is ...h6 first

■ The deeply theoretical Najdorf should not be attempted without prior study

Najdorf (Game 3)
B.Spassky-R.Fischer
World Championship,
Reykjavik 1972

1 e4 c5 2 ♘f3 d6 3 d4 cxd4 4 ♘xd4 ♘f6 5 ♘c3 a6 6 ♗g5 e6 7 f4 ♗e7 8 ♕f3 ♕c7

This is a main line Najdorf which Fischer and Spassky had not yet contested in this match. In Games 7 and 11 Fischer had played the Poisoned Pawn Variation (7...♕b6, which he had made famous with previous successes, only to fall to some excellent preparation by Spassky in Game 11 of the match—see Game 5 below).

9 0-0-0 ♘bd7

10 ♗d3

This was a relatively new move at the time. The idea behind it is to continue White's smooth development, while defending c2 and aiming a "bazooka" at h7 in case the black king castles kingside. If the black king stays in the centre then ♖he1 and the sacrifice ♘d5 becomes possible. The move which had been played most frequently in this position is 10 g4, but this was well known to Fischer from his years of experience and study of it. For a typical example with some side-variations see Najdorf Game 4.

10...b5 11 ♖he1 ♗b7

12 ♕g3

There was a brilliancy prize game, (Velimirović-Ljubojević, Yugoslav

Championship 1972), which continued 12 ♘d5 ♘xd5! (12...exd5 simply gives White too much play with 13 ♘f5! etc.) 13 exd5 ♗xg5 (13...♗xd5? 14 ♕xd5 exd5 15 ♖xe7+ wins) 14 ♖xe6+ (If 14 fxg5 then ...♘e5 followed by ♗xd5 with advantage.) 14...fxe6 15 ♘xe6 ♕a5? 16 ♕h5+ g6 17 ♕xg5 ♖g8 18 ♖d2! ♘f8 19 ♘xf8 ♕d8 20 ♘xh7 ♕xg5 21 fxg5 ♔f7 22 ♘f6 ♖h8 23 g3 ♗c8 24 h4 ♗f5 25 ♗xf5 gxf5 26 h5 ♖a7 27 ♖f2 and Black resigned. Of course there were improvements for Black (mainly recognized was 15...♕b6! instead of 15...♕a5?).

White should also have played 15 ♕h5+ instead of 15 ♘xe6, securing a draw (ref. Speelman, 1982). The text move puts considerable pressure on Black since 12...b4? would invite 13 ♘d5! with even more play for White after 13... exd5 14 e5! etc.

Hence Fischer tries to escape with his king to the queenside, sacrificing a pawn for some compensation. Today it is known that 12...h6! is an improvement for Black. If then 13 ♗h4? g5! 14 fxg5 ♘h5 15 ♕e3 ♕c5 and Black has counterplay for his pawn. On 13 ♗xf6 Black should play 13...♘xf6 (not 13...♗xf6 allowing 14 ♗xb5! etc.).

12...0-0-0

13 ♗xf6

Subsequently Velimirović (again) vs Hazzar, Nice Olympiad 1974, found 13 ♗xb5 axb5 14 ♘dxb5 ♕b6 15 e5 d5 (15 dxe5 is also bad) 16 f5! ♘h5 17 ♕h4 ♗xg5+ 18 ♕xh5 ♘xe5 19 ♕xh5 d4 20 ♖xe5 dxc3 21 ♘xc3 1-0. There may be improvements for Black in this line, but it does seem to favour White.

13...♘xf6 14 ♕xg7 ♖df8 15 ♕g3 b4 16 ♘a4 ♖hg8 17 ♕f2 ♘d7

Fischer's two bishops, together with White's disrupted piece coordination, suggest that Black has compensation for his pawn deficit.

18 ♔b1 ♔b8 19 c3 ♘c5 20 ♗c2 bxc3 21 ♘xc3 ♗f6

Fischer's excellent piece placement continues to offer compensation for his pawn, but this is not definite.

22 g3 h5 23 e5 dxe5 24 fxe5 ♗h8

Not 24...♗xe5 25 ♘db5 axb5 26 ♘xb5 ♕ moves 27 ♖xe5.

25 ♘f3 ♖d8 26 ♖xd8+ ♖xd8 27 ♘g5

There is not much else for White to do in this position, despite his pawn plus.

27...♗xe5 28 ♕xf7 ♖d7

Black could also play 28...♗xg3, e.g. 29 hxg3 ♕xg3 with equality.

Spassky should now repeat with 29 ♕e8+ ♖d8 30 ♕f7 etc. but instead he takes a great risk with...

29 ♕xh5?! ♗xc3 30 bxc3 ♕b6+

And now the exposed position of the white king proved to be a problem, especially with his queen and knight so far away.

31 ♔c1

On 31 ♔a1 ♖d2 is very dangerous for White.

31...♕a5 32 ♕h8+ ♔a7 33 a4

White is two pawns up but has a very loose position.

33...♘d3+ 34 ♗xd3 ♖xd3 35 ♔c2 ♖d5 36 ♖e4!

Spassky finds the only way to keep in the game. If now 36 ♖xg5 37 ♕d4+ and White will have excellent chances to draw.

36...♖d8 37 ♕g7 ♕f5 38 ♔b3 ♕d5+

A more deadly attempt would have been 38...♖d1 followed by ...♕f2 with a very dangerous onslaught.

39 ♔a3 ♕d2 40 ♖b4 ♕c1+ 41 ♖b2 ♕a1+ 42 ♖a2 ♕c1+ 43 ♖b2 ♕a1+

And the game is clearly drawn.

½-½

NAJDORF MASTERY LESSON 4

Pure Fischer in the "Najdorf Jungle"

■ The Najdorf is based on the deployment ...d6, ...♘f6, ...e6 ...a6, ...b5, ...♘bd7, ...♗b7 and ...♗e7

■ After 8 ♕f3 ♕c7 9 0-0-0 one of the sharpest Najdorf systems is initiated

■ This variation with ♗g5, g4 and ...b5 is one of the sharpest in the Najdorf

■ White avoids "The Jungle" and slows things down a little with 13 a3

■ Fischer defends and counterattacks via the centre to the white king

■ Open lines, combined with some creativity, ensure victory

■ The deeply theoretical Najdorf should not be attempted without prior study

Najdorf (Game 4)
D.Minić-R.Fischer
Rovinj-Zagreb, 1970

The following game is pure Fischer. It doesn't involve the typical complications which may ensue from this sharpest of Najdorf variations. Instead I would just like to point to some of the possible razor-sharp complications that may follow. By no means am I trying to present state of the art theory but I do want readers to appreciate that the Najdorf is a minefield!

1 e4 c5 2 ♘f3 d6 3 d4 cxd4 4 ♘xd4 ♘f6 5 ♘c3 a6 6 ♗g5 e6 7 f4 ♗e7 8 ♕f3 ♕c7 9 0-0-0 ♘bd7 10 g4 b5 11 ♗xf6 ♘xf6 12 g5 ♘d7 13 a3

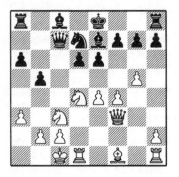

This move avoids the complications (with which Fischer was quite familiar) stemming from 13 f5 ♘c5 (Black can also play 13...♗xg5+ 14 ♔b1 ♘e5 15 ♕h5 ♕e7 16 ♘xe6 ♗xe6 17 fxe6 g6 18 exf7+ ♔xf7 19 ♕e2 ♔g7 20 ♘d5 ♕d8 =, occurring in Ervin-Gligoric, USA, 1972, and Hellers-Howell, Groningen, 1984-85) 14 f6 gxf6 15 gxf6 ♗f8

a) 16 ♕h5 ♖g8 (16...b4 17 ♘d5 exd5 18 exd5 ♗d7 19 ♖e1+ ♔d8 20 ♔b1 when White is considered slightly better (*ECO-B*)—hard to imagine what "slightly" means in a complex position such as this) 17 e5 ♗d7 18 exd6 ♗xd6 19 ♕xh7 0-0-0 20 ♕xf7 ♖df8 21 ♕h5 b4 22 ♘ce2 ♖xf6 which was unclear in the 1985 correspondence game, Costa Jr.-Consolino;

b) 16 ♖g1 b4 17 ♘d5 exd5 18 exd5 ♗d7 19 ♖g7 ♕a5 20 ♕e3+

♔d8 21 ♖xf7 ♕xa2 which again was thoroughly unclear in Doghri-Hernandez, Dubai, Olympiad, 1986;

c) 16 ♗h3 b4 17 ♘d5?! exd5 18 exd5 ♗xh3 19 ♖he1+ ♔d8 20 ♘c6+ ♔c8 21 ♕xh3+ ♔b7 when Fischer slipped away against Ciocaltea in Netanya, 1968.

13...♖b8 14 h4 b4 15 axb4 ♖xb4 16 ♗h3 0-0!

This was a new move at a time when 16...♘c5 was standard.

17 ♘f5

Now if 17 ♘xe6 fxe6 18 ♗xe6+ ♔h8 19 ♘d5 ♕c4 and Black stands better.

17...♘c5 18 ♘xe7+ ♕xe7

Again we see the simple, pragmatic, and sound approach of Fischer whose beloved Najdorf Variation has brought him to a very comfortable position.

19 h5? ♗b7

Fischer's counterplay in the centre comes just in time. If White plays 20 ♖he1 Black could continue with 20...♖b8 etc.

20 h6 ♗xe4!

Fischer judges that a knight will be more effective than a bishop on e4.

21 ♘xe4 ♘xe4 22 hxg7 ♖c8! 23 ♖h2 ♖a4 24 ♔b1 d5

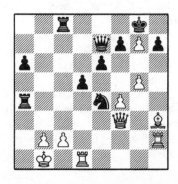

While White's attack is stalled, Fischer prepares for a final onslaught.

25 c4

25...♘c3+! was threatened.

25...♖axc4 26 ♗f1 ♖b4 27 ♕h3 ♘c3+ 28 ♔c1 ♘a4+ 29 ♔b1 ♖xb2+

Fischer has seen the end very clearly.

30 ♖xb2 ♘c3+ 31 ♔c1 ♕a3 32 ♗d3 ♕a1+ 33 ♔d2 ♕xb2+ 34 ♔e1 ♘e4 35 ♗xe4 0-1

And White is completely lost after 35...♕b4+ etc.

Najdorf (Game 5)
N.Short-G.Kasparov
PCA World Championship,
London 1993

One Najdorf System which Fischer made a "living" out of was the "Poisoned Pawn Variation". In fact 7...♕b6 became Fischer's pet move. With it, in effect, he was claiming that Black can steal a pawn, give his opponent some 3-4 moves in development, and still win!

1 e4 c5 2 ♘f3 d6 3 d4 cxd4 4 ♘xd4 ♘f6 5 ♘c3 a6 6 ♗g5 e6 7 f4 ♕b6 8 ♕d2 ♕xb2 9 ♘b3

Before Spassky-Fischer, Game 11, World Championship Match, 1972, which we will address below, the more popular move here was 9 ♖b1 forcing 9...♕a3.

9...♕a3 10 ♗xf6 gxf6

Akin to the Richter-Rauzer Variation White at least inflicts some damage on Black's pawn structure. This means that the black king will not be particularly well protected in any sector of the board.

NAJDORF MASTERY LESSON 5

Another "Najdorf Jungle"

The Poisoned Pawn Variation

■ With the "Poisoned Pawn Variation" (7...♕b6, another Fischer favourite) Black is in effect giving White 3-4 moves in development for a pawn

■The question that is always surrounding this system: "Is the black queen causing enough trouble for her loss of tempi - and will she return from her journey safely?"

■ Here Short elects to play the formerly less popular 9 ♘b3 which led Spassky to victory in Game 11 of his 1972 match against Fischer

■ With 14 ♘d1 the game diverges

■ In the Poisoned Pawn Variation Black will always lag in development, his king will usually be caught in the centre, and his rooks will not be connected

■ Short rejects a draw with 20 ♘c4; Kasparov sacrifices the exchange and gradually converts defence to an initiative

■ The deeply theoretical Najdorf should not be attempted without prior study

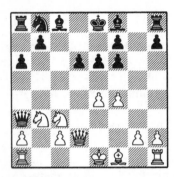

11 ♗e2

White has three minor pieces developed—to Black's none.

11...♘c6 12 0-0 ♗d7 13 ♔h1

The alternative, 13 ♗h5, is a thematic move which enables White to keep an eye on Black's weakness on f7.

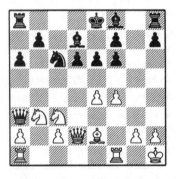

13...h5

Another continuation was 13...♖c8 14 ♗h5 ♗g7 15 ♖f3 0-0 16 ♖d1 f5 17 exf5 exf5 Am.Rodriguez-Vera, Havana 1978; Black could also try 13...♗e7 14 ♘b1 ♕b4 15 ♕e3 ♗d8 16 ♘1d2 ♕b6 17 ♕g3 and White is better.

14 ♘d1

This diverges from Spassky-Fischer, 1972, which continued: 14 ♘b1 ♕b4 (other tries for Black are: (a) 14...♕b2!? 15 a3 (15 a4 f5 is un-

clear) 15...♖c8! 16 ♖f3 e5! 17 ♘c3 ♘d4 and White appears to be in trouble; (b) 14...♕a4 15 c4) 15 ♕e3 d5? This was deemed to be Fischer's losing move in this game. Instead he could have continued as none other than his successor, Karpov, did with 15...♘e7 16 c4 f5 17 a3 ♕a4 18 ♘c3 ♕c6 19 ♘d4 ♕c5 20 exf5 ♗g7 21 fxe6 fxe6 22 ♖ad1 ♗xd4 23 ♕xd4 ♕xd4 24 ♖xd4 ♘f5 25 ♖d2 ♖c8 26 ♖f3 ♔e7 and Black is better, Jingxuan-Karpov, Hannover, 1983) 16 exd5 ♘e7 17 c4! ♘f5 18 ♕d3 h4? (Another mistake by Fischer. He was obviously having an off-day after taking a decisive lead in the match. He did not lose another game after this 11th game débâcle.) 19 ♗g4 ♘d6 20 ♘1d2 f5? 21 a3! ♕b6 22 c5! ♕b5 23 ♕c3 fxg4 24 a4! h3 25 axb5 hxg2+ 26 ♔xg2 ♖h3 27 ♕f6 ♘f5 28 c6 ♗c8 29 dxe6 fxe6 30 ♖fe1 ♗e7 31 ♖xe6 1-0.

Another game, Tal-R.Byrne, Leningrad Interzonal, 1973, continued: 14 ♕e3!? ♖c8 (on 14...♘a5 15 ♘d5! exd5 16 exd5+ ♗e7 17 ♖fe1! ♘xb3 18 ♗d3, White has the initiative) 15 ♘b1 ♕a4 (not 15...♕b2? 16 ♘1d2 b5 17 a3) 16 c4 ♘a5 17 ♕c3 (17 ♘c3? is met by 17...♕b4 18 ♖ab1 ♘xc4 19 ♕d4 ♕b6! 20 ♕xf6 ♖h6) 17...♘xc4 18 ♕xf6 ♖h6 19 ♕d4 ♖h7 20 f5, with White holding an initiative.

14...♖c8

Also possible was 14...♕b4 15 ♕e3 ♘e7 16 a3 ♕a4 17 f5 e5 assessed as unclear in Platonov-Bukhover, USSR, 1963, but Black's hold on d5 gives him a comfortable game.

15 ♘e3

Another continuation might be 15 ♖f3 ♕b4 16 ♕e3 ♕a3 17 ♕b6 ♕b4 18 ♕f2 ♕xe4 19 ♗d3 ♕a4 20 ♘b2 ♕a3 21 ♘c4 ♕b4 22 a3 ♕c3 23 ♗f1 with a winning advantage for White.

15...♕b4 16 c3 ♕xe4

Or 16...♕b6 17 ♘c4 ♕c7 18 ♖ad1 (18 ♖fd1 h4!?).

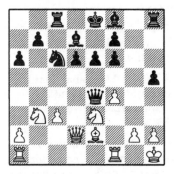

17 ♗d3

Some fantasy lines here are: 17 ♘c4 ♘d8 18 ♗d3 (18 ♘b6 ♕c6 19 ♘xc8 ♕xc8; 18 ♘d4 ♖c7) 18...♖xc4!? 19 ♗xe4 ♖xe4 and Black has two bishops and two pawns for the queen.

17...♕a4 18 ♘c4 ♖c7

Another move was 18...♖d8.

19 ♘b6 ♕a3 20 ♖ae1?

Logical was 20 ♘c4, forcing a draw by repetition.

Another continuation was 20 ♕e3 ♔d8?! 21 ♘a8 d5 22 ♕b6 ♕d6 with compensation.

20...♘e7

On 20...♔d8 there is 21 ♕f2 and 21 f5. On the other hand 21 ♘c4 ♕a4 22 ♖e4?! can be met by 22...d5!.

21 ♘c4

An interesting alternative was 21 f5 e5 22 ♗e4 ♗h6 23 ♕d3 with an unclear game; and if 21 c4 f5 (if 21...♗c6 22 ♗e4 ♗xe4 23 ♖xe4 ♖c6 24 c5 wins for White) 22 c5 d5 23 ♗xf5 ♘xf5 24 ♘xd5 ♔d8 with a slightly better game for Black.

21...♖xc4

Kasparov, ahead in the match by two points, senses that Short is indecisive, so he takes a shot at grabbing a distinct initiative. Not, however, 21...♕a4?? 22 ♘xd6+ ♔d8 23 ♘xf7+.

22 ♗xc4 h4 23 ♗d3?

Better moves were 23 ♖f3!? or 23 ♗e2! ♗g7 etc.

23...f5 24 ♗e2 ♗g7 25 c4

Another continuation is 25 ♗f3 b5 (but not 25...d5? 26 c4! dxc4 27 ♖d1) etc.

25...h3 26 g3 d5

It should be apparent that White is losing this position.

27 ♗f3?

On 27 cxd5 ♘xd5 28 ♗f3 0-0 29 ♗xd5 exd5 Black is better because of the exposed position of the white king.

27...dxc4

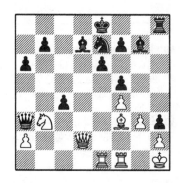

28 ♖e3

After 28 ♖d1 ♘d5 29 ♗xd5 exd5, we have the following continuations:

(a) 30 ♕xd5 ♗c6 (30...♕e7! is also good for Black) 31 ♖fe1+ ♗e5! (31...♔f8? 32 ♕xc6 bxc6 33 ♖d8 mate) 32 ♖xe5+ ♔f8 winning;

(b) 30 ♖fe1+ ♔f8 31 ♘d4 ♖h6;

(c) 30 ♘d4 ♗e6 31 ♖fe1 ♔d7 32 g4!?

28...c3

28...cxb3 29 ♖xb3 with the idea ♖xb7.

29 ♖xc3 ♗xc3 30 ♕xc3 0-0 31 ♖g1

31 g4 ♖c8 32 ♕f6 is possible.

31...♖c8 32 ♕f6 ♗c6 33 ♗xc6 ♖xc6 34 g4 ♘g6 35 gxf5 exf5 36 ♕xf5 ♕xa2 37 ♕xh3 ♕c2 38 f5

38...♖c3!

Also winning was 38...♕e4+ 39 ♕g2 ♕xg2+ 40 ♖xg2 ♖c3 41 ♘a5 ♖c1+ 42 ♖g1 ♖xg1+ 43 ♔xg1 b6 44 fxg6 bxa5.

39 ♕g4?

Or 39 ♘d4 ♕e4+ 40 ♕g2 ♕xg2+ 41 ♔xg2 ♘e5 winning.

39...♖xb3 40 fxg6 ♕c6+

Kasparov's final little combination which forces victory.

0-1

Najdorf (Game 6)
N.Short-G.Kasparov
PCA World Championship, London 1993

We will complete our section on the Najdorf Variation with the following exciting draw from the Short-Kasparov Match. It is an effective illustration of the dynamics of play for both sides. The game also illustrates some motifs from our next topic, the Boleslavsky

Structure, (with black pawns on e5 and d6, and a knight on c6) as eventually occurs in this game.

1 e4 c5 2 ␔f3 d6 3 d4 cxd4 4 ␔xd4 ␔f6 5 ␔c3 a6 6 ⍖c4 e6 7 ⍖b3 b5 8 0-0 ⍖e7 9 ⚌f3

This move was popularized in the United States in the 1970s by GM Andrew Soltis, but originates from the Soviet Union. The idea is a rapid shift of the white queen to the kingside for an attack against the black king.

9...⚌c7 10 ⚌g3 0-0 11 ⍖h6 ␔e8 12 ⌶ad1 ⍖d7

13 ␔f3!

Kasparov had introduced this move in Linares eight months earlier, against Boris Gelfand, then world No.3, and scored a spectacular victory. Before that, the main line was 13 f4 after which play can continue 13...␔c6 14 ␔xc6 ⍖xc6 15 f5 ⚍h8 16 ⍖e3 b4 17 ␔a4 ␔f6 (one alternative continuation from here was 17...⌶b8?! 18 fxe6 fxe6 19 ⌶xf8+ ⍖xf8 20 ⌶f1 ⚌e7 (only move) 21 e5 ⍖xa4 22 ⍖g5 ⚌a7+ 23 ⍖e3 ⚌e7 24 ⍖xa4 Sokolov-Gelfand, USSR Championship 1989, when White was clearly better and won in 64 moves) 18 fxe6

␔xe4 19 ⚌h3 fxe6 20 ⚌xe6 ⍖f6 21 ⚌c4 ⚌b7 22 ␔b6 ⌶ae8 23 ⚌xb4 ⍖xb2 24 ⍖d5 Damaso-Arnason, Novi Sad Olympiad 1990, which was drawn in 61 moves.

The other main move for Black after 13 f4 is 13...⚍h8 14 ⍖g5 ⍖xg5 (or 14...␔c6 15 ⍖xe7 ␔xe7 16 f5 e5 17 ␔e6 fxe6 18 fxe6 ⌶xf1+ 19 ⌶xf1 ␔f6 20 exd7 ⚌xd7 21 ⚌d3 ⌶d8 22 g3 h6 Tischbierek-Gruenberg, East German Championship, Zittau, 1989, ending in a draw in 23 moves) 15 ⚌xg5 ␔c6 16 ␔xc6 ⍖xc6 17 f5 ␔f6 18 fxe6 fxe6 19 ⍖xe6 ⚌a7+ 20 ⚍h1 ␔xe4 21 ␔xe4 ⍖xe4 22 c3 ⌶f2 23 ⌶xf2 ⚌xf2 24 ⍖d5 Sieiro-Vera, Cuban Championship 1982, drawn in 26 moves; another alternative for Black is 13...b4. The game, I.Almasi-Vaulin, Kecskemet 1993, continued 14 ␔ce2 ⚍h8 15 ⍖g5 ␔c6 16 f5 ␔xd4 17 ␔xd4 ␔f6 18 ⚌h4 ⌶ae8 19 fxe6 fxe6 20 ⍖xe6 ⍖d8 21 ⚌h3 ⌶xe6 22 ␔xe6 ⚌b6+ 23 ⚍h1 and, with 23...⌶e8 to follow, the game was drawn.

More passive is 13 a3 ␔c6 14 ␔xc6 ⍖xc6 15 ⌶fe1 (15 f4 ⍖f6 16 f5 ⚌e7 17 ⚌g4 ⚍h8 18 ⍖d2 ⍖xc3 19 ⍖xc3 e5 20 ⌶fe1 ␔f6 21 ⚌h4 ⌶ad8 22 ⌶d3 ⚌b7 23 ⌶de3 ⌶fe8 24 h3 Stirenkov-Vaulin, Budapest 1991, but White stood slightly better and won in 41 moves. The 20th and final game of the Short-Kasparov match, again with Kasparov as Black, continued 15 ⍖f4 ⚌b7 16 ⌶fe1 a5 17 e5 dxe5 18 ⍖xe5 ⍖f6 19 ⌶d4 ⌶d8 20 ⌶xd8 ⍖xd8 21 ␔e2 a4 22 ⍖a2 b4 23 axb4 ⚌xb4 24 ⍖c3 with White holding an initiative but the game ending in a draw in 36 moves.)

Two examples in this line continued 15...a5 16 f3 (the move 16 ♗g5 was tested in the game Riegler-Danner, Ljubliana 1993, 16...♗xg5 17 ♕xg5 ♕b7 18 ♖d4 ♘f6 19 ♕e3 ♖fd8 20 ♖ed1 b4 21 axb4 e5 22 ♖4d3 ♕xb4 23 f4 exf4 24 ♕xf4 when White was slightly better and won in 44 moves). 16...♗f6 after which 17 ♗g5 ♗xg5 18 ♕xg5 ♘f6 19 ♕g3 ♖fd8 20 ♖d2 a4 21 ♗a2 b4 22 axb4 ♕b6+ 23 ♕f2 ♕xb4 24 ♘d1, with an equal position in Martin del Campo-Sunye Neto, Merida 1993.

13...a5!
This was Kasparov's own improvement on 13...b4!? as played against him by Gelfand, a game which is fully annotated in my book *Practical Middlegame Techniques* (Everyman, 1997).

That game continued 14 ♘e2 a5 15 ♘f4! ♔h8 16 ♗g5 ♘f6 17 ♕h4! ♗b5? (on 17...a4 18 ♘h5 axb3 19 ♘xf6 White is better; 17...♘c6 deserves attention) 18 ♘d4! ♗e8 (if 18...♗xf1 19 ♘dxe6 fxe6 20 ♗xe6 g6 21 ♘xg6+ ♔g7 22 ♕h6 mate) 19 ♘dxe6! fxe6 20 ♘xe6 ♕a7 21 e5! dxe5 22 ♘xf8 ♗xf8 23 ♗xf6 gxf6 24 ♖d8 ♘d7 25 ♕g4! 1-0 (Kasparov-Gelfand, Linares,1993).

Another completely sound move for Black is 13...♘c6!? after which three game continuations were:

(1) 14 ♗g5 ♗xg5 15 ♘xg5 ♖d8 16 f4 h6 17 ♘f3 b4 18 ♘e2 ♘f6 19 e5 ♘e4 20 ♕h4 dxe5 21 fxe5 ♘c5 22 ♕g3 ♗c8 23 ♖xd8 ♖xd8 24 ♔h1 with Black slightly better in Sax-Wojtkiewicz, Budapest 1993, and eventually winning in 42 moves.;

(2) 14 ♗f4 ♖d8 15 ♖fe1 ♗c8 16 h4 ♔h8 17 ♖d3 Zapata-Sunye Neto, Merida 1993, when Black is equal;

(3) 14 ♘e2 a5 15 c3 a4 16 ♗c2 e5 17 ♘d2 ♗e6 18 ♗b1 ♔h8 19 ♗e3 ♘f6 20 f4 ♘h5 21 ♕f3 ♘xf4 22 ♘xf4 exf4 23 ♕xf4 a3 24 b3, Ashley-Arnason, Saint Martin,1993, and Black should have little to fear since he has weakened White's queenside and has excellent chances due to his access to the e5 square.

14 a4 b4 15 ♘e2 ♘c6 16 ♘f4 ♗f6?!
It seems that Kasparov could have forced play more with 16...♔h8 17 ♗g5 h6 18 ♗xe7 ♘xe7 when Black's position is clearly very solid.

17 ♘d3
17 ♘h5 ♗xb2 18 e5 ♘xe5! 19 ♗xg7 ♘xf3+ 20 gxf3 ♗xg7 wins.

17...e5

An important principle to remember in this structure is that when White's knights do not have access to the d5 or f5 squares then ...e5 is most likely to be a strong move.

18 ♗e3 ♗e7 19 ♘d2 ♘f6 20 f3

On 20 f4 ♘g4 gives Black play.

20...♖fe8 21 ♔h1 ♗e6

Black's solid centre suggests that he has little to fear.

22 ♖fe1 ♖ac8

Now Black can play 22...d5, e.g.,

(a) 23 ♗g5!?

(b) 23 ♘c5? ♗xc5 24 ♗xc5 d4 25 ♗xe6 ♖xe6 26 ♖e2 ♘d7 27 ♘b3 ♘d8 28 ♗xd4 ♖g6 winning;

(c) 23 exd5 ♘xd5 and Black is very solid again.

23 ♕f2 d5!

With this move Black achieves classic Sicilian equality.

24 ♗b6 ♕b8 25 ♗c5 ♗xc5

After 25...d4?! 26 ♗xe6 fxe6 27 ♗xe7 ♖xe7, White stands slightly better.

26 ♘xc5 ♘d4 27 ♘xe6 fxe6 28 exd5

28...♘xb3

This move avoids the tremendous complications which could follow on 28...exd5 29 ♘e4! (after 29 f4 ♘xc2 30 ♖xe5 ♖xe5 31 fxe5 ♕xe5 Black is better) 29...♘xb3 (not 29...♘xe4? 30 ♗xd5+ ♔h8 31 ♗xe4 winning) 30 ♘xf6+ gxf6 which, after further great complications stemming from 31 ♖xd5 (which we will omit), is at least equal for Black.

29 ♘xb3 exd5 30 ♘xa5 ♕a8 31 ♘b3 ♕xa4 32 ♖a1 ♕c6 33 ♖e2 d4

And the game was agreed drawn, enabling Kasparov to retain his title by a margin of 12½ to 7½. Play could have continued 34 ♖a5 (on 34 ♖ae1 ♘d5 35 ♖xe5 ♖xe5 36 ♖xe5 ♕xc2 37 ♕xc2 ♖xc2 38 ♖xd5 ♖xb2 39 h4 ♖xb3 40 ♖xd4=) 34...♕d6 35 ♕e1 d3 36 cxd3 ♕xd3 37 ♘c5 ♕d4=

½-½

Notes for this game are based on references kindly provided by GM Lubomir Ftačnik in *ChessBase*.

B. The Boleslavsky Variation

We have already discussed the Sicilian Boleslavsky Structure characterized by black pawns on d6 and e5, against a white pawn on e4. Strictly speaking, in modern times the Boleslavsky Variation is said to occur when White plays 6 ♗e2 after the opening sequence 1 e4 c5 2 ♘f3 ♘c6 3 d4 cxd4 4 ♘xd4 ♘f6 5 ♘c3 d6 and Black follows with ...e5. However similar positions and structures can occur from various opening move sequences by either player. Let us look at some typical examples of games which illustrate the Boleslavsky Variation at its best.

BOLESLAVSKY MASTERY LESSON 1

The "Fischer Boleslavsky"

- The Boleslavsky Variation arises when White plays 6 ♗e2 against the Najdorf

- Black will use the setup ...d6, ...♘f6, ...a6, ...e5, ...♗e6, ...♗e7, ...♕c7, ...♘bd7

- Black should strive for queenside counterplay with ...b5

- Black should try to control the d5 square and play ...d5

- When Black is able to play ...d5 without incurring any specific weaknesses, he usually at least equalizes

- If White plays a4-a5 Black should play for ...b5 anyway

- After axb6 he must be wary of a weak a-pawn

Boleslavsky (Game 1)
W.Unzicker-R.Fischer
Varna Olympiad 1962

The undeniable master of the Boleslavsky/Najdorf formation was Bobby Fischer, and here his short victory against Wolfgang Unzicker was exemplary for his deep understanding of this system. Unzicker was poorly prepared and not aware of an important improvement which

Geller had found on move 15 for White. Not only did Fischer have problems against Geller in this variation, but he had problems against Geller in general.

1 e4 c5 2 ♘f3 d6 3 d4 cxd4 4 ♘xd4 ♘f6 5 ♘c3 a6 6 ♗e2 e5
Fischer has often demonstrated that Black can live with his backward d-pawn thanks to the possibility of queenside expansion, pressure on e4 and excellent central control in general.
7 ♘b3 ♗e6
More flexible is 7...♗e7; the text move aims to provoke f4.
8 0-0 ♘bd7 9 f4 ♕c7 10 f5 ♗c4 11 a4
White tries to restrain Black's queenside counterplay.·
11...♗e7 12 ♗e3 0-0 13 a5 b5!
Black must strive for immediate counterplay, otherwise White will quickly carry out g4-g5 with a crush.
14 axb6 ♘xb6

15 ♗xb6?
This is where Geller improved with 15 ♔h1! ♖fc8 16 ♗xb6 ♕xb6 17 ♗xc4 ♖xc4 18 ♕e2 ♖b4 19 ♖a2! when Black's a-pawn becomes

a problem. Zuckerman has suggested 19...h6 20 ♖fa1 ♗f8 21 ♖xa6 ♖xa6 22 ♖xa6 ♕b7 23 ♘a5 ♕c7 24 ♘b3 ♕b7 with equality (Reference: *My 60 Memorable Games*, by Robert Fischer, p.267).

15...♕xb6+ 16 ♔h1 ♗b5!

Preparing ...♗c6 and ...a5.

17 ♗xb5 axb5 18 ♘d5 ♘xd5 19 ♕xd5 ♖a4!

An important feature of this game is White's inability to control d5 with his knight. This is not accidental. It is all part of Fischer's Najdorf System.

20 c3 ♕a6

Black increases the pressure.

21 h3

Tal-Fischer, Curaçao 1962, continued 21 ♖ad1 ♖c8 22 ♘c1 b4 (the classic Sicilian minority attack) 23 ♘d3?! bxc3 24 bxc3 and now 24...♖xc3 (instead of 24...♖a5) would have won for Black, e.g. 24...♖xc3 25 ♘xe5 dxe5 26 ♕xe5 ♗b4 27 ♕xc3 ♕xf1+ (Kmoch).

21...♖c8 22 ♖fe1 h6!

This takes care of any back rank problems.

23 ♔h2 ♗g5 24 g3 ♕a7 25 ♔g2 ♖a2 26 ♔f1 ♖xc3 0-1

One conclusive line is 27 ♖xa2 ♖f3+ 28 ♔g2 ♕f2+ 29 ♔h1 ♖xg3.

**BOLESLAVSKY MASTERY
LESSON 2**

The "Theoretical Najdorf"

■ The Boleslavsky Variation arises when White plays 6 ♗e2 against the Najdorf

■ Although play may initially start out as a Scheveningen, a genuine Boleslavsky may arise by transposition (e.g. ...♘xd4, ...♘d7, ...e5, f5, etc

■ Black should try to control the d5 square and play ...d5

■ At an opportune moment Black may exert pressure on the c-file to play ...♖xc3. The gain of a pawn, with this exchange sacrifice shattering White's queenside, usually represents sufficient compensation

■ Black may then revert to the "queenside-kingside swipe"

Boleslavsky (Game 2)
R.Hübner-V.Anand
Dortmund 1996

The following game illustrates themes which are very typical in the realm of the Boleslavsky. True, the opening starts out in the family of the Najdorf or Scheveningen, but as the pawn structure transforms into a Boleslavsky proper, we see the game develop into an exciting Sicilian classic.

1 e4 c5 2 ♘f3 d6 3 d4 cxd4 4 ♘xd4 ♘f6 5 ♘c3 a6 6 ♗e2 e6

At this point we have a Najdorf move order leading to a Scheveningen.

7 0-0 ♗e7 8 f4 0-0 9 ♗e3 ♘c6 10 ♕e1

As we've seen in Game One of the Scheveningen Mastery lessons, this is all mainstream.

10...♘xd4 11 ♗xd4 b5 12 a3 ♗b7 13 ♗d3 ♘d7

Black prepares his counter with ...e5.

14 ♖d1 ♕c7 15 ♔h1 e5 16 ♗e3 ♖ac8 17 ♕g3 ♗f6

So far normal play by both sides, but it seems that White's attack is being thwarted.

18 f5 ♔h8 19 ♖f2 ♗e7

Here we see the structural dynamism of the Scheveningen/ Boleslavsky: White can only get an attack on the kingside with g4-g5 but this is hard to accomplish and in the meantime Black can play for the levers ...d5 and/or ...b4.

20 ♖fd2 ♕a5 21 ♕e1

As we have mentioned earlier, after ♘d5, ♗xd5, exd5, the resulting pawn structure will always favour Black.

21...h6 22 h3 ♘f6 23 ♗f2

23...♖xc3! 24 bxc3 ♕xa3

The thematic Sicilian exchange sacrifice. White's e-pawn is weak as are his c-pawns. Black has continuing play on the half-open c-file and, with a pawn for the exchange, he will have more than enough compensation.

25 c4 bxc4 26 ♗xc4 ♘xe4 27 ♖d3 ♕a4

Now 28 ♗d5 would allow 28...♗xd5 29 ♗xd5 ♕xc2 with a decisive material and positional advantage.

28 ♖b3 ♕xc4 29 ♖xb7 ♕xc2 30 ♗g1 ♗g5 31 ♖db1 ♗f4

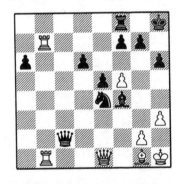

32 ♖1b3 d5 33 ♖f3 ♖c8 34 ♖xf7 ♘g5 35 ♖xf4 exf4 36 ♖e7 f3 0-1

After, for example, 37 ♖e8+ ♔h7 38 gxf3 ♕xf5 39 ♖xc8 ♕xf3+ 40 ♔h2 ♕xh3 mate follows.

BOLESLAVSKY MASTERY LESSON 3

The "Classic Boleslavsky"

■ The Boleslavsky Variation arises when White plays 6 ♗e2 against the Najdorf

■ If White plays the opening passively Black may find an opportune moment to play ...d5 and steal the initiative

■ In the ensuing play Black obtains a mobile kingside majority and destroys White's queenside structure

■ Black's play on the half-open c-file, coupled with his mobile majority, ensures victory

■ Black may then revert to the "queenside-kingside swipe", especially if White's back rank is weak and his defenders are offside

Boleslavsky (Game 3)
Y.Kosashvili *White*
A.Greenfeld *Black*
Israeli League, Tel Aviv 1999

From Black's perspective, the following is a very typical game with the Boleslavsky. Black has few problems in the opening and finds a way to wrest the initiative in the transition from the opening to the middlegame.

1 e4 c5 2 ♘f3 ♘c6 3 d4 cxd4 4 ♘xd4 ♘f6 5 ♘c3 d6 6 ♗e2 e5 7 ♘b3 ♗e7 8 0-0 0-0

This could be viewed as a very typical opening sequence in the Boleslavsky Variation. There are few dangers for Black.

9 ♗f3 a5

Black quickly initiates play on the queenside, securing the b4 square for his queen's knight which helps to support ...d5.

10 a4 ♘b4 11 ♗g5 ♗e6 12 ♗xf6 ♗xf6 13 ♘d2

White hopes to continue along positional lines by ♖e1, ♘f1 and ♘e3 with a grip on the light squares. However Black will not allow this.

13...♖c8 14 ♘db1

White fears the possible positional exchange sacrifice ...♖xc3, followed by ...♘a2.

14...d5 15 exd5 ♗f5 16 ♘a3 e4

Now any capturing sequence on e4 will end with ...♗xb2 and Black is winning.

17 ♗g4 ♗xg4 18 ♕xg4 ♗xc3!

A very sharp continuation which provides Black with a lasting structural edge and an initiative.

19 bxc3 f5 20 ♕g3 ♘xd5!

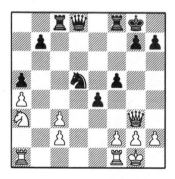

White cannot now play either rook to d1 since Black has 21...♘xc3!, winning after 22 ♖xd8 ♘e2+.

21 ♘b5 ♕f6 22 c4 ♖xc4 23 ♕b3 ♖c5

Black has correctly calculated that the pin of his ♘d5 is not serious.

24 ♖ad1 ♕e6 25 ♖fe1 ♔h8

Black prepares an onslaught which will feature the advance of his kingside majority.

26 ♘d4 ♕f6 27 ♕xb7 ♘c3 28 ♖d2 f4

Already a decisive ...e3 is menaced.

29 ♕a7 ♖g5

Now the white king is threatened directly.

30 ♘b5 e3

On 31 fxe3 ♘e4! 32 ♖ moves f3! is devastating for White.

31 ♖d3

31...♘e2+

A wonderful clearance move that is the beginning of the end for White.

32 ♔f1 ♖xg2

On 33 ♔xe2 ♖xf2+ 34 ♔d1 ♕a1 is mate!

33 ♖xe2 ♕a1+ 34 ♔xg2 f3+ 35 ♔h3 ♕f1+ 36 ♔h4 fxe2 37 ♕f7

White probably hoped this would save him, but Black has an answer...

37...♕xf2+ 0-1

5: The Kan Structure and its Relatives

The Kan variation or structure of the Sicilian Defence is based on the moves ...a6, ...e6 and ...♕c7. In itself the structure is full of holes.

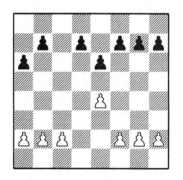

In this variation Black sets out by staking his claim to the light squares with pawn moves such as ...e6, ...a6, and possibly later also ...b5. Then Black proceeds to catch up in development and control of the dark squares, and more terrain in general, by ...♕c7, followed by ...♘f6, ...♘c6, ...♗b4 and ...♗b7.

The variation is direct and almost naive in its apparently simplistic approach to contesting the centre. In the main variations Black may develop his king's bishop to b4 with an assault on the white knight on c3, thereby challenging White's centre and e-pawn. From c7, probably the most pertinent square for the black queen in the Sicilian Defence, the queen eyes d6, e5, and the entire b8-h8 diagonal, as well as offering play on the half-open c-file. It offers many transpositional opportunities to the Scheveningen if Black later plays ...d6, ...♗e7, ...0-0 and usually ...♗b7; but in the Kan Black usually has to delay castling longer than in the Scheveningen. He may, in some lines, initiate an attack on the white king before he castles.

A. Kan Variation

The Kan Variation is based on the early sequence of moves, ...e6, ...a6, ...♕c7, etc. A typical opening with the Kan Variation might go:

1 e4 c5 2 ♘f3 e6 3 d4 cxd4 4 ♘xd4 a6 5 ♘c3 ♕c7

The basic Kan setup.

6 ♗e2 ♘f6 7 0-0 ♘c6

Variation I

8 ♗e3 ♗b4 9 ♘a4
The usual reply is...
9...0-0
....as 9...♘xe4? 10 ♘xc6 ♕xc6 11 ♘b6 followed by ♕d4 gives White too much.
10 ♘xc6 bxc6 11 ♘b6
Now White will gain the two bishops and a pawn, but in return for trading off his knight, which has moved four times, for a bishop which has not moved at all!
11...♖b8 12 ♘xc8 ♖fxc8 13 ♗xa6 ♖f8! 14 ♕d3 ♘g4 15 g3 ♕a5

Black seems to have excellent compensation for the a-pawn, Hübner-Ribli, Germany, 1987.

Another main line 8th move continuation for White here is:

Variation II

8 ♔h1

Black has two main lines:

Line 1: 8...♘xd4 9 ♕xd4 ♗c5 10 ♕d3 b5 11 f4 h5

This is a typical move for Black in the Kan Variation. Lagging in development, Black must look for unusually aggressive measures. The naïvely direct approach of the Kan Variation shows itself here. Black can ill afford any more pawn moves to contest the centre (i.e. ...d6 which would also cut off his king's bishop) so he just develops aggressively.
   If instead 11...♗b7 12 ♗f3 b4 13 e5 gives White an advantage; while after 12...0-0 13 e5 ♘e8 14 ♘e4 ♗e7 15 a4 is clearly better for White, as in Stoica-Gavrilakis, Skopje 1984.
   12 e5 ♘g4 13 ♕g3 ♗b7
After 14 ♗xg4 hxg4 15 ♕xg4 Black would naturally castle long with excellent attacking chances.
   14 ♗f3
White, for his part, takes control of as much of the centre as possible.
   14...0-0-0 15 a4 !
Notice how, in a number of Kan continuations, this thematic lever gives White the better chances. The text was played in Zapata-Marjanović, Titograd, 1984.

   A second continuation for Black here is:

Line II: 8...♗b4

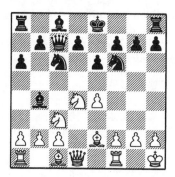

9 ♘xc6

Another idea for White is 9 ♗g5 ♗xc3 10 ♗xf6 gxf6 11 bxc3. This position is considered to favour White because Black's kingside is weakened and he lags behind in the development of his queenside. Yet Black could gradually bring himself back into the game with ...d6, ...♗d7, and ...♖c8.

9...bxc6 10 f4

Now Black can mix things up with 10...♗xc3 11 ♗xc3 ♘xe4 when White can reply with either 12 ♕d4 or 12 ♗a3. On 12 ♕d4 ♘f6 appears necessary and then 13 ♗a3 would be a natural continuation giving Black real problems on the a3-f8 diagonal. 12 ♗a3 is not so convincing as Black can continue with 12...c5.

10...0-0 11 e5 ♗xc3 12 bxc3 ♘d5

This occurred in Renet-Taimanov, Montpellier 1986, and is considered unclear. White seems unable to maintain a bind on the a3-f8 diagonal without further pawn sacrifices

The following game is an early example of what this Chapter is all about. It was played by none other than Louis Paulsen who is credited

with Black's whole system of play coupling ...e6 and ...a6 with ...♘c6 and ...♕c7 (currently better known as the Kan Variation). You will see elements of the various Sicilan Systems we have discussed—the backward black d-pawn, the development of the black king's bishop to b4, the knight deployment ...♘c6 and ...♘ge7 with ...♘ec6 to follow, and ...a6, ...b5 followed by an opposite wing attack.

Kan (Game 1)
J.Zukertort-L.Paulsen
Frankfurt 1887

1 e4 c5 2 ♘c3 ♘c6 3 f4 e6 4 ♘f3 ♘ge7 5 d4 cxd4 6 ♘xd4 ♘xd4 7 ♕xd4 ♘c6 8 ♕f2 ♗b4 9 ♗d2 d6 10 0-0-0 0-0 11 ♘b5

This move seems to be the source of White's problems for the rest of this game, as the knight costs him much time.

11...♗c5 12 ♕g3 e5 13 ♗c3 ♕e7 14 f5 a6 15 ♘a3 b5 16 ♘b1 ♗b7 17 ♗d2 ♔h8 18 ♗g5 f6 19 ♗e3 ♕f7 20 ♘c3 ♘d4 21 ♗d3 b4 22 ♗xd4 ♗xd4 23 ♘d5 ♗xd5 24 exd5 ♕xd5 25 ♔b1 ♕c5 26 h4 d5 27 ♗e2 e4 28 ♕b3 a5 29 ♕a4 ♖fc8 30 ♖h3 ♗e5 31 ♗b5 ♖c7 32 ♗d7 e3 33 ♖c1

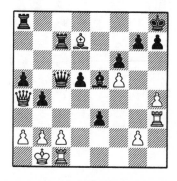

33...♕d4 34 c3 ♕d3+ 35 ♕c2 ♕xc2+ 36 ♖xc2 ♖xd7 37 ♖xe3 bxc3 38 bxc3 ♖b8+ 0-1

The following game shows some of the typical tensions inherent in the Kan system. The notes are based on those of Tiviakov and Donev.

Kan (Game 2)
S.Tiviakov-L.Milov
Groningen 1998

1 e4 c5 2 ♘f3 e6 3 d4 cxd4 4 ♘xd4 a6 5 ♘c3 ♕c7 6 ♗d3 ♘c6

This variation had become a favourite of V.Milov.

7 ♘xc6 dxc6

Black recaptures this way to maintain a balanced pawn structure, apart from the hole created on b6. If instead 7...bxc6 8 f4 d6 9 e5!? and Black might run into difficulties completing his development.

8 0-0 e5 9 f4 ♘f6 10 ♔h1 ♗d6 11 f5 b5

Modern theory assesses this variation to be in White's favour. This may well be correct but the position remains very complex and difficult to play for both sides.

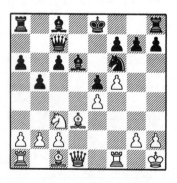

12 a4

12 ♗g5 is an alternative and sometimes leads merely to a transposition of moves. After 12...♗b7 (Black doesn't need to develop his king's bishop immediately although Mamadshoev-Nijboer, Yerevan 1996 continued 12...♗e7 13 a4 ♗b7 14 ♕f3 h6 15 ♗e3 0-0 16 b3 ♗b4 17 ♘d1 c5 18 c3 c4 19 bxc4 bxc4 20 ♗c2 ♗c5 21 ♘f2 ♖ab8 22 ♖ab1 ♗a8 23 g4 ♘d7 24 h4 ♖xb1 25 ♖xb1 ♖b8 26 ♖xb8+ ♕xb8 27 ♘d1 ♗xe3 28 ♕xe3 ♔f8 ½-½) 13 a4 ♗c5 (13...♗e7 leads us to the position after 12...♗e7 13 a4 ♗b7) 14 ♕e2 h5, White stands better, although later he failed to convert his advantage into something more tangible: 15 ♘d1 ♖d8 16 ♖f3 ♕d6 17 ♖h3 ♕d4 18 ♗e3 ♕d6 19 ♗g5 ♕d4 20 ♕e1 ♖d7 21 ♗e3 ♕d6 22 ♖g3 ♗xe3 23 ♘xe3 ♕d4 24 ♖xg7 ♘xe4 25 ♖d1 ♘f6 26 axb5 axb5 27 c3 ♕f4 28 ♖g3 e4 29 ♗c2 ♖xd1 30 ♗xd1 ½-½ Tiviakov-Miezis, New York 1998. After that game an improvement was prepared, 12 a4, which was tested against the same opponent seven months later...

12...♗b7!

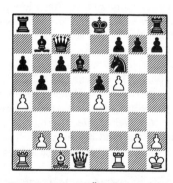

On 12...b4? 13 ♘b1 White has a large advantage due to his control of the c4 square. The second

Tiviakov-Miezis game, Port Erin
1998, went 13...h5 14 ♘d2 a5 15
♕e1 ♗c5 16 ♘f3 ♔f8 17 b3 ♗b7
18 ♗b2 ♖e8 19 ♕g3 ♗d6 20 ♖ad1
♕e7 21 ♗c1 ♗c5 22 ♘g5 h4 23
♕h3 ♔g8 24 ♗c4 and White won.
12...♖b8 is stronger than 12...b4,
but nevertheless this move is not
necessary if Black can play
12...♗b7. A quick draw was agreed
in Gallagher-Dizdarević, Suhr 1990,
after 13 ♗e3 ♕e7 14 ♕f3 ♘d7 15
♕h5 ♘f6 16 ♕g5 ♔f8 17 ♕h4 h6
18 g4 ♔g8 19 ♖g1 ♗b7 20 g5
½-½.

13 axb5!?

After the game Tiviakov felt there
were two possibly better
alternatives, 13 ♕e2 and 13 ♗g5!?,
transposing into 12 ♗g5 ♗b7 13 a4,
retaining the better chances for
White in both cases.

**13...axb5 14 ♖xa8+ ♗xa8 15
♗xb5 cxb5**

This is a sacrifice which Black
has to accept.

16 ♘xb5 ♕c6

On 16...♕c5 17 ♕xd6 (17
♘xd6+? ♔e7 is bad for White,
since he loses the knight on d6)
17...♕xb5 leads us to the same position as after 16...♕c6 17 ♕xd6
♕xb5.

17 ♕xd6

17 ♘xd6+? ♔e7 is losing for
White.

17...♕xb5

The only move. The ending after
17...♕xd6 18 ♘xd6+ ♔e7 19 ♘c4
♗xe4 (19...♖c8? 20 ♘b6 wins) 20
♘xe5 ♗xc2 21 ♗g5! is very bad,
probably lost for Black.

18 ♖d1

Stronger than 18 c4?! ♕d7!? 19
♕xe5+ ♕e7 (19...♔f8!? is also
interesting).

18...♘d7

Black doesn't have any choice
and has to make forced moves to the
end of the game.

19 ♗g5 f6 20 ♕e6+

20 ♗xf6 gxf6 21 ♕e6+ doesn't
transpose into the text, since Black
has 21...♔f8! at his disposal, exploiting the weakness of the first
rank.

20...♔d8

20...♔f8 21 ♕xd7 ♕xd7 22 ♖xd7
♔e8 23 ♖a7 ♗xe4 24 ♗e3 is bad
for Black.

21 c4

The critical position of the game.
It took more than an hour for
Tiviakov to make this move. At first
he was going to play 21 ♗xf6+ at
once but then became attracted by
21 c4, failing to notice the text
move, 23...♔c7. After he found it,
he wasted a lot of energy searching
for a forced win. When it became
clear that 21 c4 leads only to a
draw, Tiviakov had less than 30
minutes to the time-control and was
exhausted by the calculations. A
very sharp and unclear position
arises after 21 ♗xf6+ gxf6
(21...♔c8 22 ♗xg7 is lost for
Black) 22 ♕xf6+ ♔c7 23 ♕xh8.
Here Black has a choice between

23...♗xe4 and 23...♕e2. Even after the analysis it's difficult to say which move is stronger.

To illustrate here are some variations:

(a) 23...♗xe4!? (threatening 24...♗xg2+ 25 ♔xg2 ♕e2+) 24 ♕g8 (24 ♕g7 ♗xf5 is unclear) 24...♗xf5 is also unclear (24...♕e2!?);

(b) 23...♕e2

(b1) 24 ♖c1 ♗xe4 and 25...♗xf5 (24...♕d2!? and 25...♗e4 also deserves attention) ;

(b2) 24 ♖a1 ♗xe4 25 ♕g7 (25 ♕g8 ♗xf5 is unclear) 25...♗xf5 is unclear since White is unable to keep both queenside pawns.

21...♕c6

Everything is forced. All other moves lose. For example: 21...♕a4 22 b3 ♕c6 (22...♕a7 23 ♗e3) 23 ♖d6 ♖e8 (23...♕b7 24 ♗e3 wins, e.g. 24...♔c8 25 ♖d5 ♖d8 26 ♖c5+ ♔b8 27 ♖b5) 24 ♖xc6 ♖xe6 25 ♖xe6 fxg5 26 b4 see the variation after 21...♕c6 22 ♖d6 ♖e8 23 ♖xc6 ♖xe6 24 ♖xe6 fxg5 25 b4; 21...♕b7 22 ♗e3 ♔c8 (22...♖e8 23 ♗b6+ decides) 23 ♖d5! winning.

22 ♖d6

22 ♗e3 is met by 22...♔c7.

22...♕a4 23 ♗e3 ♔c7 24 b3

24 ♖a6? is bad after 24...♕d1+ 25 ♗g1 ♗b7, followed by ...♖a8 (25...♗xe4 26 ♖a7+ ♔b7 and 27...♖a8 is also possible).

24...♕a1+ 25 ♗g1 ♖d8

26 ♖xd7+

This is the simplest, but not the only way to force the draw. 26 ♖a6 is an alternative, e.g. after 26...♕d1 27 ♖a7+ ♔b7 28 c5 or 27 c5 would eventually lead to a draw.

26...♖xd7 27 ♕b6+ ♔c8 28 ♕c5+ ♔b8

Black can't escape from the checks, e.g. 28...♔d8 29 ♕f8+ ♔c7 30 ♕c5+ ♗c6 31 ♕b6+ =; 28...♖c7 29 ♕f8+ ♔d7 30 ♕f7+ ♔d8 31 ♕f8+ ♔d7 32 ♕f7+ ♔c8 33 ♕e8+ ♔b7 34 ♕b5+ =.

29 ♕b5+

And a draw was agreed here, bringing an end to a very interesting game.

½-½

B. The Taimanov Variation

GM Mark Taimanov is a Soviet Grandmaster I have always appreciated because he is an original thinker who is not afraid to experiment and find his own innovations. Rather than call this or that sequence of moves "the Taimanov" I would credit him with a variety of systems of play which are somewhere between the Scheveningen and the Kan Variations. Taimanov, for example, is credited with 1 e4 c5 2 ♘f3 e6 3 d4 cxd4 4 ♘xd4 ♘c6 5 ♘c3 ♕c7. He is also credited with variations involving ...♘ge7 in conjunction with the idea of ...♘xd4 and ...♘c6.

Furthermore his name is attached to lines which stem from the Kan Variation (...e6, ...a6, ...♕c7 and ...♘c6).

Incidentally, after being crushed 6-0 by Bobby Fischer in the 1971 Candidates Semi-final, not many players would be able to console themselves, as he did, by saying, "Well at least I have my music!" Taimanov is also a concert pianist.

Taimanov (Game 1)
A.Karpov-G.Kasparov
World Championship,
Moscow 1985

In the 16th Game of his 1985 world title re-match with Anatoly Karpov, Garry Kasparov introduced a pawn sacrifice which resulted in the finest game of the contest, exemplifying superb board control from beginning to end. The pawn sacrifice came out of a Taimanov System.

1 e4 c5 2 ♘f3 e6 3 d4 cxd4 4 ♘xd4 ♘c6 5 ♘b5 d6

In this position Fischer crushed Taimanov in continuations stemming from 6 ♗f4 e5 etc.

6 c4 ♘f6 7 ♘1c3 a6 8 ♘a3

Normal in this position are 8...♗e7 or 8...b6. In either case Black ends up fianchettoing his queen's bishop and playing a type of "Hedgehog System", defined by the row of pawns on a6, b6, d6 and e6.

8...d5!

9 cxd5 exd5 10 exd5 ♘b4 11 ♗e2

Subsequent examples are:

(a) 11 ♗c4 ♗g4 (11...b5? 12 0-0) 12 ♕d4 (12 ♗e2 ♗xe2 13 ♕xe2+ ♕e7 occurred in Game 12, Karpov-Kasparov 1985, and led to an equal ending) 12...b5 13 ♘cxb5 (after 13 ♗b3 ♗c5 14 ♕e5+ ♔f8 Black is slightly better) 13...axb5 14 ♗xb5+ ♗d7 15 d6 which was unclear in Jadoul-Varnusz, Budapest, 1985, and Santo Roman-Kouatly, Cannes, 1986;

(b) 11 ♕a4+ ♗d7 12 ♕b3 ♗c5 is considered unclear.

11...♗c5

An important improvement for White is 12 ♗e3! ♗xe3 13 ♕a4+, which occurred in Karpov-Van der Wiel, Brussels, 1986, with White holding an edge.

12 0-0 0-0 13 ♗f3 ♗f5

From here Kasparov embarks on a policy of restriction which he does not relinquish for the rest of the game.

14 ♗g5 ♖e8 15 ♕d2 b5

Black is uninterested in regaining the d-pawn. Instead he aims to limit the movement of White's pieces. Notice that the white knights cannot move, nor has his king's bishop much mobility.

16 ♖ad1 ♘d3

This invasion further constricts White while threatening ...b4.

17 ♘ab1 h6 18 ♗h4 b4 19 ♘a4 ♗d6

Again White's knights cannot move.

20 ♗g3 ♖c8 21 b3 g5 22 ♗xd6 ♕xd6 23 g3 ♘d7

Karparov regroups and works around the d5 pawn.

24 ♗g2 ♕f6 25 a3 a5 26 axb4 axb4 27 ♕a2 ♗g6 28 d6 g4 29 ♕d2 ♔g7 30 f3 ♕xd6

Finally Kasparov converts to some tactics based on his tremendous positional advantages.

31 fxg4 ♕d4+ 32 ♔h1 ♘f6 33 ♖f4 ♘e4 34 ♕xd3 ♘f2+ 35 ♖xf2 ♗xd3 36 ♖fd2 ♕e3 37 ♖xd3 ♖c1

38 ♘b2 ♕f2 39 ♘d2 ♖xd1+ 40 ♘xd1 ♖e1+

And White is mated.

0-1

Taimanov (Game 2)
G.Orlov-M.Taimanov
St Petersburg, 1995

1 e4 c5 2 ♘f3 e6 3 d4 cxd4 4 ♘xd4 ♘c6 5 ♘c3 a6 6 ♗e2 ♘ge7

This is one of the Taimanov Systems I have alluded to above. Mark Taimanov is a supreme master of the ...♘ge7 system which he invented and practised for many years.

7 ♘b3

If White doesn't move this knight, then Black will usually exchange it. However, the question is which knight is more useful: the white one on b3 or the black one on g6?

7...b5 8 0-0 ♘g6

The flexibility of this knight for both defensive and offensive purposes is remarkable. If White plays f5, Black's knight will have a haven on e5.

9 f4 ♗e7 10 ♗e3 0-0 11 ♗d3 ♘b4

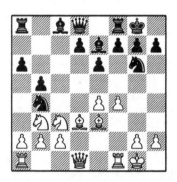

Another typical move by Taimanov in his own system. He strongly believes in the potential of the two bishops—yet he is flexible enough to play with knights against bishops if the position demands it.

12 ♕h5 ♘xd3 13 cxd3 f5

Immediately setting about opening the diagonal for his queen's bishop.

14 ♘d5

A cute combination which Taimanov is able to ignore. If 14...exd5? 15 exf5 followed by f6 and ♕xd5+ is White's idea.

14...♗b7 15 ♘xe7+

At first it is hard to comprehend why Orlov doesn't play 15 ♗b6 but presumably he feared 15...♕b8 16 ♘c7 fxe4 17 ♘xa8 ♗xa8 when Black has excellent compensation for the exchange. Such ploys are typical of Taimanov's play and he often uses them to extricate himself from difficult positions.

15...♘xe7 16 ♘c5 ♗c6 17 ♗d4 ♕e8 18 ♕g5 ♕f7

Now it is clear that Black has a very defensible, solid position.

19 ♖f3 h6 20 ♕g3 ♔h7 21 ♖c1 ♖g8

Suddenly Taimanov shows that he has no fear of playing ...g5.

22 ♕e1 d6 23 ♘b3 ♖ac8 24 ♗c3 ♗a8 25 ♖f2

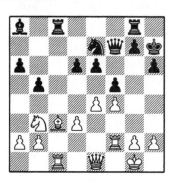

25...♕g6 26 ♖e2 ♖gf8 27 ♕h4 ♖f7 28 ♖ce1 ♖cf8 29 ♘d2 fxe4 30 ♘xe4 ♘f5

Taimanov achieves all his positional goals—a wonderful queen's bishop and a knight planted on f5. White must also live with a weak pawn on d3.

31 ♕h3 ♔g8 32 ♘g3 ♗d5 33 a3

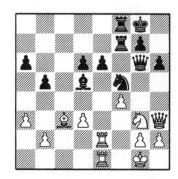

33...a5 34 ♘e4 b4 35 axb4 axb4 36 ♗xb4 ♘d4 37 ♖f2 ♖xf4 38 ♖xf4 ♖xf4

All of Black's pieces are very active.

39 ♗xd6 ♖f3 40 ♗g3 ♖xd3

The ♘e4 is undermined.

41 ♘c3 ♘f5

Finally Black wins a pawn as a result of the pin of the bishop on g3.

42 ♘xd5 exd5 43 b4 ♔h7 44 ♖f1 ♘xg3 45 hxg3 ♖xg3 46 ♕h2 ♖g5

White's pawn on b4 is now lost, leaving Black with a won game.

47 ♕h3 ♕b6+ 48 ♖f2 ♕xb4 49 ♕d3+ ♔g8 50 ♖e2 ♕c5+ 51 ♔h2 ♖h5+ 52 ♔g3 ♕d6+ 53 ♔g4 ♖g5+ 54 ♔h3 ♕g6 55 ♕xg6 ♖xg6 56 ♖d2 ♖g5 57 g4 ♔f7 58 ♔g3 h5 59 ♔h4 ♔g6 60 gxh5+ ♖xh5+ 61 ♔g4 ♖e5 0-1

Taimanov (Game 3)
Sofia Polgar-M.Taimanov
London Foxtrot 1996

1 e4

This battle between the veteran Taimanov and young Sofia Polgar promised an interesting struggle.

1...c5 2 ♘f3 e6 3 d4 cxd4 4 ♘xd4 ♘c6 5 ♘c3 a6 6 ♗e3 ♘xd4 7 ♕xd4 ♘e7

It is interesting to see how Taimanov manages to deal with the weakness on d6.

8 f4 b5 9 0-0-0 ♘c6 10 ♕d2 ♗e7

Taimanov starts out modestly, with preventive defence.

11 ♕f2 ♗b7 12 g4 0-0 13 ♗g2 ♕c8 14 ♗c5 ♗xc5 15 ♕xc5

White is playing very consistently, striving to exploit the backward black d-pawn and d6 square. Taimanov finds ways to defend and sticks to basic Sicilian themes for counterplay.

15...♘a5 16 ♕xc8 ♗xc8!

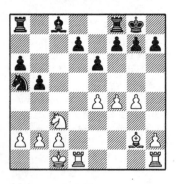

Taimanov is not afraid to resort to innocuous means to defend—see how his game improves in less than ten moves!

17 ♖d3 ♖a7 18 ♖hd1 ♖c7 19 b3 f6

Another preventive move.

20 h4

This seems to overextend White's position.

20...♘c6 21 a4?

The losing move.

21...♘b4 22 ♖h3 bxa4 23 bxa4 ♗b7 24 ♖d4 a5 25 ♗f1 ♖fc8 26 ♔b2 d5

Black now has more than equality.

27 exd5 ♘xd5 28 ♘b5 ♖xc2+ 29 ♔b3 ♘xf4 30 ♖c3 ♖2xc3+ 31 ♘xc3 ♘d5 32 ♘e4 ♘e3 33 ♘d6 ♖d8 34 ♗c4 ♗d5! 0-1

Black either wins more material or simplifies to a winning ending.

6: Offbeat Systems and a Repertoire

As you develop your skill in the Sicilian Defence do not be afraid to explore and learn a few systems well. The first four chapters of this book have covered the main systems of play which are regularly seen in master and grandmaster praxis. However, the element of surprise is very important in any competitive endeavour, especially between opponents of equal strength. I therefore recommend that you develop a "bread and butter" Sicilian repertoire based on one of the solid systems, such the Scheveningen, and then cultivate some secondary systems which you can use on special occasions for variety, experimentation and surprise. You'll be amazed how few people will want to engage you in main line theory because they, like you, fear that their opponents may be "completely booked up". Here are a few lesser-known Sicilian Systems which I recommend that you explore. They may not fully equalize with best play, but they are sharp and tend to throw off all but the best-prepared opponents.

A. The O'Kelly Variation: 2...a6

The main idea behind this variation is that Black can play a fast ...e5 after, for example, 3 d4 cxd4 4 ♘xd4 e5 (or 4 ...♘f6 followed by 5...e5) with a very playable game. The most effective lines against this system for White are regarded as 3 c3 and 3 c4 after which the move 2...a6 may prove to be irrelevant and a loss of time.

The game below is not an O'Kelly Variation proper, since Black does not play 2...a6, but it pursues the same theme. It illustrates Mark Taimanov (again!) at his best. After losing a pawn, he persists with active positional ideas—including the superiority of his centrally posted knight over a relatively passive bishop. Eventually he is rewarded and scores a full point against the then World Champion.

A.Karpov-M.Taimanov
Leningrad, 1977

1 e4 c5 2 ♘f3 ♘c6 3 d4 cxd4 4 ♘xd4 a6 5 c4 e5 6 ♘b3 ♘f6 7 ♘c3 ♗b4 8 f3 0–0 9 ♗e3 d6 10 ♖c1 b6 11 ♗d3 ♗c5 12 ♕d2 ♗e6 13 ♘xc5

bxc5 14 0–0 ♘d4 15 ♘d5 ♘d7 16
f4 ♖b8 17 f5 ♗xd5 18 cxd5 ♕b6
19 ♖f2 f6 20 ♖c4 a5 21 ♖a4 ♖a8
22 ♕e1 ♖a7 23 b3 ♖fa8 24 ♖b2
♕c7 25 ♗d2

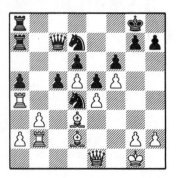

25...♘b6 26 ♖xa5 c4 27 ♗f1
♖xa5 28 ♗xa5 ♕c5 29 ♗xb6
♕xb6 30 ♔h1 cxb3 31 axb3 g6 32
fxg6 hxg6 33 b4 ♔g7 34 b5 f5 35
exf5 ♘xf5 36 ♖b3 ♕d4 37 b6 ♖a1
38 ♖b1 ♘g3+ 0-1
If 39 hxg3 ♖a8 and ... ♖h8 mate.

B. The Lowenthal
(or Labourdonnais) Variation

This variation is as old as it is
sharp and basic. For players who
like a sharp, open game it is an excellent weapon to be occasionally
employed, particularly for surprise
value. The fact that Black quickly
creates a very backward d-pawn and
relinquishes its primary defender,
the dark-squared bishop, is subordi-
nate to Black's desire for quick development. In most variations Black
sidesteps the issue of his backward
d-pawn by quickly advancing it to
d5, even as a gambit! The main
point is that Black seeks fast devel-

opment with active play. Such tactics may throw the player of the
White pieces off-balance early. I
would not recommend this system
to be played against opponents who
are over 2400 Elo rating, but otherwise it is an excellent weapon to
have in one's "occasional
repertoire".

The game below illustrates the
Black style of play I am recom-
mending, but it also happens to be a
wonderful example of how rook and
bishop can be superior to rook and
knight. Fischer's active use of his
king in the endgame is particularly
noteworthy—although the outcome
has little to do with the opening.

R.Fischer-M.Tal
Curaçao Candidates, 1962

1 e4 c5 2 ♘f3 ♘c6 3 d4 cxd4 4
♘xd4 e5 5 ♘b5 a6 6 ♘d6+ ♗xd6
7 ♕xd6 ♕f6 8 ♕d1 ♕g6 9 ♘c3
♘ge7 10 h4 h5 11 ♗g5 d5 12
♗xe7 d4 13 ♗g5 dxc3 14 bxc3
♕xe4+ 15 ♗e2 f6 16 ♗e3 ♗g4 17
♕d3 ♕xd3 18 cxd3 ♗xe2 19 ♔xe2
0-0-0 20 ♖ad1 ♘e7 21 d4 ♘d5 22
♖c1 ♖he8 23 ♖hd1 f5 24 ♗g5 ♖d7
25 dxe5 ♖xe5+ 26 ♔f3 ♖e4

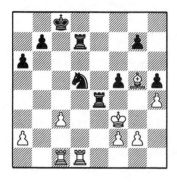

27 ♖d3 ♖c4 28 ♖cd1 ♖xc3 29 ♖xc3+ ♘xc3 30 ♖c1 ♖c7 31 ♗f4 ♖c6 32 ♗e5 ♘d5 33 ♖d1 ♘f6 34 ♔f4 g6 35 f3 ♘d7 36 ♗d6 ♖c2 37 g3 ♖e2 38 ♔g5 ♖e6 39 ♗f4 ♘f8 40 ♖d6 a5 41 ♔h6 ♖e2 42 ♖d2 ♖e7 43 ♗d6 ♖h7+ 44 ♔g5 ♖f7 45 ♖b2 f4 46 ♗xf4 ♖f5+ 47 ♔h6 b5 48 ♗d6 b4 49 g4 ♖xf3 50 g5 ♘e6 51 ♔xg6 ♖d3 52 ♗e5 ♖e3 53 ♔f5 ♘f8 54 ♖g2 ♖f3+ 55 ♗f4 ♔d7 56 g6 ♘e6 57 g7 ♖xf4+ 58 ♔e5 ♖f8 59 gxf8=♕ ♘xf8 60 ♔d5 a4 61 ♖g7+ ♔e8 62 ♔d6 b3 63 axb3 1–0

C. Nimzovich Variation (2 ...♘f6)

The positive features of this variation are:

(1) there are few ways for White to gain a clear advantage other than the long, narrow variation given here;

(2) there are not many openings where Black can force the white king to remain in the centre and lose his castling rights.

1 e4 c5 2 ♘f3 ♘f6 3 e5 ♘d5 4 ♘c3 e6 5 ♘xd5 exd5 6 d4 ♘c6 7 dxc5 ♗xc5 8 ♕xd5 ♕b6

8...d6 is an interesting alternative which can lead to further complications after 9 exd6 ♕b6 etc.

9 ♗c4 ♗xf2+ 10 ♔e2 0–0 11 ♖f1 ♗c5 12 ♘g5 ♘d4+ 13 ♔d1 ♘e6 14 ♘e4 d6

White may have an advantage, but it requires very precise play. How many of your opponents would know the best line(s) for White?

7: Closed Systems

For purposes of discussion, I will define any Sicilian where White does not play 1 e4, 2 ♘f3 and 3 d4 as a "Closed System". These are not really so hard to identify and I think they share one thing in common: *Black is given the chance to play positionally and can choose from a number of viable setups.* In other words, Black is not put under great immediate pressure and can try to develop soundly and safely. I will try to make some suggestions and give examples of exactly what this means. The essential premise is that Black has done nothing wrong, and so, with a sober and careful approach, sticking to the basic principles of opening play, he should be able to equalize. It is important that Black addresses the strategic themes which White poses, though of course these themes may not always be so obvious.

In this chapter I will review a number of such systems for White, including:

A. The Closed Sicilian proper, where White usually plays 2 ♘c3, coupled with d3, g3, ♗g2, etc.

B. The Grand Prix Attack where White plays e4 and f4, threatening a quick and dangerous kingside attack.

C. The c3 Sicilian Variation in which White plays 2 c3, hoping for an early d4 with a big centre and chances of a kingside attack.

D. The Kopec System in which White plays 2 ♘f3 and 3 ♗d3.

E. Closed Systems with ♗b5, e.g., 1 e4, 2 ♘f3 and 3 ♗b5 against 2...♘c6.

My feeling about all these systems is that they should not create major problems for the Sicilian Defence if Black plays logically. Sure, it helps to know specific variations and have some experience with them, but none of these systems, in themselves, should be so dangerous for Black that he cannot contest the centre, get developed, and be able to castle safely without incurring any long-term weaknesses. In this Chapter I will try to illustrate some of Black's best ways of meeting "Closed Systems". These examples are taken largely from my own personal experience and after studying them I hope that readers will have sufficient knowledge to face any Closed System against the Sicilian Defence with confidence and a sense of security.

A. The Closed Sicilian

In my experience, I have found that many opponents choose the Closed Sicilian for White because they fear that Black is well booked up on the Open Variations. As far as I am concerned this has never really been the case. I know a few variations quite well, largely from experience, but I have never been a book specialist. Furthermore, as the reader should have surmised from the style of this book, I don't worry too much about specific moves in a specific position but prefer to concentrate on patterns, themes, and goals. Admittedly, in some games I have come unstuck but by and large it has been to my advantage to know the difference between a good, sound, opening sequence and one which is destined for failure for Black.

It all has to do with *knowing and believing*. When my opponent chooses to play the Closed Sicilian for White, I am very reassured to have at least two good systems up my sleeve and the strong belief that these can lead to a very good position for Black, regardless of what White does. Equally importantly, I feel comfortable with the plans, goals, and strategic themes which are inherent in such systems.

The following game shows that players have been winning Closed Sicilian games in a similar way for well over a hundred years! It also helps to explain why it is more usual (and more dangerous for Black) for White to play 3 d4.

CLOSED SICILIAN MASTERY LESSON 1

■ **The setup ...♘c6, ...e6, ...♘ge7, and ...d6 against the Closed Sicilian is very solid for Black**

■ **When White plays c4 with e4 the d4 square becomes vulnerable to Black forces**

■ **A knight safely posted on e5 against a bad light-squared bishop which is locked behind its pawns, can be the dominant factor in a position**

■ **Superior "activity" features can transfer from the opening to the middlegame to the ending**

Closed Sicilian (Game 1)
P.Saint Amant-H.Staunton
Match, London 1843

Here we will see Black playing according to sound principles, controlling the key central dark squares with his minor pieces and pawns. His choice of the setup ...d6, ...e6 is most flexible. Following a mini-combination on move 11, Black finds a series of exchanges which lead to a superior knight vs. bishop position, after which he demonstrates excellent technique. Black's doubled d-pawns may look ugly but they prove unassailable.

1 e4 c5 2 c4

The weakness of White's d4 is already evident.

2...e6 3 ♘c3 ♘e7 4 d3 ♘bc6 5 ♗e3 ♘g6 6 f4 d6 7 ♘f3 ♗e7 8 a3 ♗f6 9 ♗e2 0-0 10 0-0 ♗d4 11 ♕d2

11...♘xf4 12 ♘xd4 cxd4 13 ♗xf4 e5 14 ♘d5 exf4 15 ♕xf4 ♗e6 16 ♕g3 ♗xd5 17 cxd5 ♘e5 18 ♖f2 ♖c8 19 ♗g4 ♖c5 20 ♖af1 ♕g5 21 h3 ♖c1 22 ♔h2 ♖xf1 23 ♖xf1 ♕d2 24 ♖f2 ♕e1 25 ♖c2 ♕b1 26 ♖d2 g6 27 ♕f2 h5 28 ♗d1 ♕c1 29 g4 hxg4 30 hxg4 ♕xd1 31 ♖xd1 ♘xg4+ 32 ♔g3 ♘xf2 33 ♔xf2 ♖c8 34 ♖d2 ♔g7 35 ♔f3 ♖c1 36 ♖h2 ♔f6 37 ♖h8 ♖d1 38 ♔e2 ♖b1 39 ♔f3 ♖xb2 40 ♖e8 ♖b6 41 e5+ dxe5 42 ♔e4 ♖d6 43 ♖xe5 ♖d7 44 ♔xd4 g5 45 ♖e1 g4 46 ♔c5 ♔g5 47 d6 f5

Black wins a close and hotly contested ending knowing that a rook plus connected passed pawns beat a single passed pawn.

48 ♖e7 ♖d8 49 ♔d5 ♔f4 50 d7 g3 51 ♖g7 ♔f3 52 ♔e5 g2 53 ♔e6 f4 54 d4 ♔f2 55 d5 g1=♕ 56 ♖xg1 ♔xg1 57 ♔e7 ♖xd7+ 58 ♔xd7 f3 59 ♔c7 f2 60 d6 f1=♕ 61 d7 ♕d3 62 d8=♕ ♕xd8+ 63 ♔xd8 b5 64 ♔c7 a5 65 ♔b6 b4 66 a4 b3 67 ♔xa5 b2 68 ♔a6 b1=♕ 69 a5 ♕b4 0-1

Closed Sicilian (Game 2)
V.Smyslov-M.Botvinnik
World Championship,
Moscow 1954

The setup Black choses against the Closed Sicilian (pawns on ...c5, ...d6 and ...e5 with ...♘c6 and ...♘ge7 and kingside fianchetto) is extremely reliable against nearly all Closed Sicilian Variations. It is known as the "Russian setup" since so many players from the former Soviet Union have been schooled in it. The main idea is that White is prevented from playing an easy d4 while Black can prepare, as appropriate, ...d5 or ...f5.

1 e4 c5 2 ♘c3 ♘c6 3 g3 g6 4 ♗g2 ♗g7 5 d3 d6 6 ♘ge2 e5 7 ♘d5 ♘ge7 8 c3

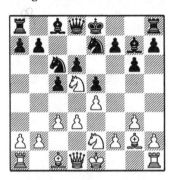

This move already lets Black get the upper hand in the middlegame pawn structure which ensues. Black, with a potential duo on e5 and f5, will always feel more comfortable. White should probably play 8 c4 instead and hope to recapture on d5 with cxd5. In that case Black may be less prone to trading knights on d5.

8...♘xd5 9 exd5 ♘e7 10 0-0 0-0 11 f4 ♗d7 12 h3 ♕c7 13 ♗e3 ♖ae8 14 ♕d2 ♘f5

Botvinnik finds an easy way to complete his development without ...f5.

15 ♗f2 h5 16 ♖ae1 ♕d8 17 ♔h2 ♗h6

Clearly Black is the aggressor. Note how useless the white minor pieces are here.

18 h4 ♕f6 19 ♗e4 exf4 20 ♘xf4

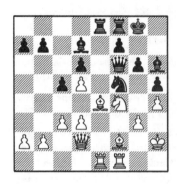

20...♘xh4

Now the game is essentially over.

21 ♗e3 ♘f5 22 ♗xf5 ♕xf5 23 ♕g2 ♕g4 24 ♕e2 ♕xe2+ 25 ♖xe2 ♖e5

The rest is simple technique for Botvinnik. Black's position seems to play itself.

26 ♖ee1 ♖fe8 27 ♗f2 h4 28 ♖xe5 ♖xe5 29 d4 hxg3+ 30 ♔xg3 ♖g5+ 31 ♔h2 ♖f5 32 ♗e3 cxd4 33 cxd4 ♔h7 34 ♖f2 g5 35 ♘e2 ♖xf2+ 36 ♗xf2 f5

Two connected passed pawns and two bishops—it's not too early for White to resign.

0-1

CLOSED SICILIAN MASTERY LESSON 3

■ The "Russian Setup" ...♘c6, ...d6, ...e5, ...♘ge7, and ...♗g7 against nearly all Closed Sicilian structures is very solid for Black

■ Here Kasparov plays ...♘f6 instead of ...♘ge7 with some alternate motifs

■ In the Closed Sicilian Black often plays ...b5 and ...♖b8

■ Here ...♖b8 regains a pawn and gains the half-open b-file

■ When White plays f4 and recaptures with a piece on f4, Black can use the d4 and e5 squares as outposts. There is little White can do against this structure

Closed Sicilian (Game 3)
M.Adams-G.Kasparov
Linares 1999
(Notes based on those of Donev and Hecht)

What follows is an amazing struggle between two of the world's very best players. Kasparov does not, strictly speaking, choose the Russian setup for Black, deviating with 6...♘f6 which has less to recommend it.

After a brutal boardwide battle, in which neither player blinks, Adams apparently misses a drawing combination and Kasparov finally emerges the victor in a courageous and subtle ending.

1 e4 c5 2 ♘c3 d6 3 g3 ♘c6 4 ♗g2 g6 5 d3 ♗g7 6 ♗e3 ♘f6 7 ♘ge2 0-0 8 h3 e5 9 0-0

9...b5!?
Another game, Farkas-Zagrebelny, Hungary 1993, continued 9...♘d4 10 ♔h2 ♗e6 11 f4 ♕d7 12 ♘d5 ♗xd5 13 exd5 ♘xe2 14 ♕xe2 exf4 15 ♗xf4 ♘h5 16 c3 ♖fe8 17 ♕f3 ♘xf4 18 gxf4 ♗e7 19 ♖ae1 ♖ae8 20 ♕f2 ♔f8 21 ♖e4 f5 22 ♖ee1 ♗f6 23 a3 ♕b5 24 ♕d2 ♗h4 25 ♖xe7 ♖xe7 26 ♗f3 ♕e8 27 b4 b6 28 ♔g2 ♖e3 29 bxc5 bxc5 30 ♖b1 ♗e1 31 ♕c2 ♕e7 32 c4 ♕h4 33 ♖xe1 ♖xe1 34 ♕b2 ♔f7 35 ♕b7+ ♕e7 36 ♕b2 ♔g8 37 ♕b8+ ♔g7 38 ♕b2+ ♕f6 39 ♕b7+ ♖e7 40 ♕b1 h5 41 ♕b8 h4 42 ♕c8 ♕b2+ 43 ♔f1 0-1.

10 ♘xb5 ♖b8 11 a4 a6 12 ♘a3 ♖xb2 13 ♘c4 ♖b8 14 f4 exf4 15 ♘xf4
If 15 ♗xf4 ♘e8 16 ♖b1 ♗e6 with equal chances.

15...♘a5 16 ♘d2 ♗d7 17 ♖a2 ♗c6
Black's setup is unusual but seems to work.

18 ♘f3 ♗a8 19 c4 ♘d7 20 ♖af2 ♘b3 21 h4 ♘d4 22 ♗h3 ♘xf3+ 23 ♕xf3 ♘e5

Black has essentially played the Russian setup, despite the fact that he developed his king's knight on f6, later transferring it via d7 to e5. Black's pawn centre is modest but it offers excellent prospects of outposts on d4 and e5.

24 ♕d1 ♕e7 25 h5 ♖b4 26 h6 ♗h8

After 26...♗xh6 27 ♘xg6 28 ♗xh6 ♖xf2 29 ♖xf2 ♖b8 the game would be equal.

27 ♘e6 ♖fb8 28 ♘g5 ♖b2

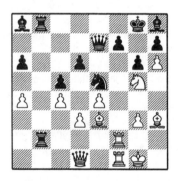

29 ♗f4

Adams misses a draw with the combination 29 ♖xf7 ♘xf7 30 ♗e6 ♗f6 31 ♕g4 ♖b1 32 ♘xf7 ♖xf1+ 33 ♔xf1 ♖e8 34 ♘g5+ ♔h8 35 ♘f7+ etc.

29...♗f6 30 ♘f3 ♗c6 31 ♘xe5 ♗xe5 32 ♕f3 f5

Clearer for Black was 32...♖xf2 33 ♖xf2 ♗d4 34 ♗e3 ♗xe3 35 ♕xe3 ♗xa4 winning a pawn.

33 ♗xe5 ♕xe5 34 g4 ♖xf2 35 ♖xf2 ♖b1+ 36 ♗f1

If 36 ♔g2 ♖b3 37 gxf5 ♖xd3!!.

36...♖b2 37 ♖xb2 ♕xb2 38 gxf5 ♕d4+ 39 ♔h1 ♗xa4 40 fxg6 hxg6

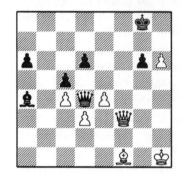

41 e5 ♕xe5 42 ♕b7 ♗e8 43 ♗g2 ♕h5+

43...a5 44 ♗d5+ ♔h8 45 ♗e6 ♗c6+ 46 ♕xc6 ♕xe6 is slightly better for Black.

44 ♔g1 ♕xh6 45 ♕e7

White could equalize with 45 ♕d5+ ♗f7 46 ♕xd6 ♕e3+ 47 ♔h2 ♔g7 48 ♗d5 ♗xd5 49 cxd5.

45...♕c1+ 46 ♗f1 ♗f7 47 ♕xd6 ♕e3+ 48 ♔h1 a5 49 ♕d8+ ♗e8 50 ♗g2

If 50 ♕xa5? ♗c6+ 51 ♗g2 (51 ♔h2 ♕f4+ 52 ♔g1 ♕g3+ 53 ♗g2 ♕xg2 mate) 51...♕h3+ 52 ♔g1 ♕xg2 mate.

50...♕e1+ 51 ♔h2 ♕e5+ 52 ♔h3 ♔g7 53 ♗d5 a4 54 ♕b6 ♗d7+ 55 ♔g2 ♕e2+ 56 ♔g1 a3 57 ♕xc5 ♕e1+ 58 ♔g2 a2 59 ♕d4+ ♔h7 0-1

CLOSED SICILIAN MASTERY LESSON 4

■ The setup with ...♘c6, ...e6, ...d6, ...♘ge7, and ...♗g7 against the Closed Sicilian is very solid for Black

■ Black often plays an early ...♘d4, possibly in conjunction with ...♘ec6

■ Black may then start queenside counterplay with ...♖b8 and ...b5, ...b4, etc or as in this game he may play ...b6

■ With ...d6 Black may play ...d5 or ...e5 at an opportune moment

■ This setup assures Black of at least an equal share of the centre

Closed Sicilian (Game 4)
N.Short-P.Leko
Wijk aan Zee 2000

The following game illustrates my favourite setup for Black against the Closed Variation. Basically it involves the moves ...c5, ...♘c6, ...e6, ...♘ge7, ...g6, and ...♗g7 in conjunction with ...d6 (or ...d5) as circumstances may dictate.

1 e4 c5 2 ♘c3 ♘c6 3 g3 g6 4 ♗g2 ♗g7 5 d3 d6 6 ♘ge2 e6 7 ♗e3 ♘d4 8 0-0 ♘e7 9 ♕d2 0-0

I have had many games with this setup and feel that it is Black, rather

than White, who is the aggressor as he is fully prepared for any attempt by his opponent to play f4 and f5.

10 ♖ae1 ♖b8 11 ♘d1 b6 12 ♘c1 d5 13 c3 ♘dc6 14 ♗h6 dxe4 15 ♗xg7 ♔xg7 16 ♗xe4 ♗b7 17 ♘e3 ♕c7 18 f4 ♖bd8 19 ♕f2

19...♘f5

Although after this move Black has few difficulties, I feel that if Black is indeed playing for a win he should try 19...f5 20 ♗g2 e5 21 fxe5 ♘xe5 when Black's superior central control and space must give him an advantage.

20 ♘xf5+ exf5

For the rest of the game Black is clearly not worse, but neither does he have enough of an advantage to win.

21 ♗f3 ♘e7 22 ♕e2 ♖d7 23 ♕e5+ ♕xe5 24 ♖xe5 f6 25 ♖e3 ♗xf3 26 ♖fxf3 ♔f7 27 a3 ♖fd8 28 ♔f1 ♘d5 29 ♖e2 ♘c7 30 ♔e1 c4 31 ♔d2 ♘e6 32 ♔c2 b5 33 b4 a5 34 dxc4 bxc4 35 ♖ff2 axb4 36 axb4 ♘c7 37 ♖d2 ♘b5 38 ♖xd7+ ♖xd7 39 ♖d2 ♖xd2+ 40 ♔xd2 ♔e6 41 ♘e2 ½-½

CLOSED SICILIAN MASTERY LESSON 5

■ The setup with ...♘c6, ...e6, ...d6, ...♘ge7, and ...♗g7 against the Closed Sicilian is very solid for Black

■ The drawback of ...♘f6 for Black is his inability to contest the f5 square with a move like f5

■ A good measure of Black's success in the opening is how effective is White's advance f5

■ Black often plays an early ...♘d4, possibly coupled with ...♘ec6

■ Black also usually plays ...♖b8 with ...b5 and ...b4 to follow

Closed Sicilian (Game 5)
G.Lane-D.Kopec
Lloyds Bank Masters, London 1977

What follows is a remarkable example of how reasonable the Closed Sicilian is for Black. True, I mishandle it with 9...♘f6 and get into trouble because I don't control the f5 square sufficiently, but Black's position is still essentially sound. Somehow I was able to impose my will on the young Gary Lane, finding a way to defend against his kingside onslaught and wrest the initiative for a pawn. It was the beginning of a necessary run of scoring 2½ from 3 possible points en route to achieving my second IM

norm, including a second win that summer (as White in a Closed Sicilian!) against GM Miguel Quinteros.

1 e4 c5 2 ♘c3 ♘c6 3 g3 g6 4 ♗g2 ♗g7 5 d3 e6 6 ♗e3 ♘d4 7 ♘ce2 d6

Black should not play 7...♘xe2?! 8 ♘xe2 ♗xb2 9 ♖b1 ♗g7 10 ♗xc5 d6 11 ♗b4 when White has a pretty distinct advantage.

8 c3 ♘c6 9 ♕d2 ♘f6?

This move does not show much foresight. Why I diverted from the usual ...♘ge7 I don't know. Certainly on 10 d4 Black can follow with 10...cxd4 11 cxd4 d5 etc. But at least I am in good company (see Adams-Kasparov, above!)

10 h3 ♖b8 11 f4 b5 12 a3 ♗b7 13 g4 ♘d7 14 ♘f3

The problem with Black's setup is the lack of control of f5 which he achieves with the ...♘ge7 system.

14...a5 15 0-0 0-0 16 ♘g3 b4 17 axb4 axb4 18 f5 bxc3 19 bxc3

Black has successfully opened lines on the queenside, but White's attack on the kingside is clearly more dangerous as was demonstrated by Spassky in three consecutive 1968 Candidates match game victories with White in the Closed Sicilian! Here I have even more play (in terms of open lines) on the queenside than Geller ever achieved, but White's attack is already very dangerous.

19...exf5

Better was 19...♘ce5.

20 gxf5 ♘ce5 21 ♗h6 ♗xh6 22 ♕xh6 ♕f6 23 ♘h2 g5 24 ♕h5 ♘xd3

It is important that Black snatches at least a pawn in return for the suffering he is about to endure on the kingside.

25 ♘g4 ♕g7 26 f6 ♕g6 27 ♖f5 ♘f4 28 ♕xg5 ♘xg2 29 ♔xg2 ♖fe8

Black threatens ...♖xe4 etc.

30 ♕f4 ♔h8 31 ♖e1?

White loses his nerve. He should force Black to prove his counterplay after 31 ♖g5 ♖xe4 32 ♘xe4 ♕xe4+ 33 ♕xe4 ♗xe4+ 34 ♔g1 when Black does not have sufficient compensation for the exchage. So you could say I was a bit lucky here!

31...♘e5 32 ♘xe5 dxe5 33 ♖xe5 ♖g8 34 ♖g1

34...♗c8!

Black finds a way to activate his forces and exploit the relatively exposed position of the white king.

35 ♔f3 ♗xh3

Finally Black re-establishes material equality and it is clear that the white king and pawns are exposed.

36 ♘e2 ♗g2+ 37 ♔e3 ♖b6

Fortunately the pinned black bishop has an influence on the white king.

38 ♖f5 ♖e6 39 e5 ♖ge8

Threatening 40 ♕xf5! 41 ♕xf5 ♖xe5+ etc. with a probable win for Black in the ending.

40 ♔f2 ♖g8 41 ♔e3 ♖ge8 42 ♘g3 ♗h3 43 ♖h5

Clearly the black bishop is in trouble and Black does not want to stumble into 43...♗g4 44 ♖g5 ♕xg5 45 ♕xg5 ♖xe5+ 46 ♕xe5 ♖xe5+ 47 ♔f4 when White wins. So what can Black do?

43...c4!

A spectacular idea, but is Black for real now or is he bluffing?

44 ♖xh3

If 44 ♕e4 ♕xh5 45 ♘xh5 ♖xe5.

44...♖xe5+

After 44...♕d3+ 45 ♔f2 ♖xe5 46 ♔g2 the white king is able to slip away.

45 ♔f3 ♕d3+

If now 46 ♔f2 ♖e2+ wins for Black; but 46 ♔g2! ♕d5+ (nor is 46...♖e3 sufficient here) 47 ♔h2 ♖e2+ 48 ♘xe2 ♖xe2+ 49 ♔g3 and again the white king slips away.

46 ♔g4 ♖g8+ 47 ♔h4 ♕g6!

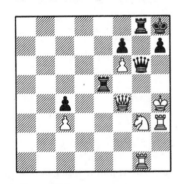

48 ♖h2 ♖g5 49 ♔h3 ♖g4 50 ♕d6 ♕g5

Black inches closer to the white king and now has a decisive attack.

51 ♖f2 ♕h4+ 0-1

CLOSED SICILIAN MASTERY LESSON 6

■ The setup with ...♘c6, ...e6, ...d6, ...♘ge7, and ...♗g7 against the Closed Sicilian is very solid for Black

■ Black often plays an early ...♘d4, possibly coupled with ...♘ec6

■ Black also usually plays ...♖b8 with ...b5 and ...b4 to follow

■ White should not spend his time fighting Black on the queenside (e.g. a3 and c3) when Black will gain time in addition to open lines in that board sector

■ It is always important for Black to consider levers to destroy White's attempts at establishing a big centre

---

Closed Sicilian (Game 6)
P.Howe-D.Kopec
Manodnock Marathon 1991

The following two games illustrate why I am very fond of this setup for Black. Black's game is so inherently sound that he is able to wrest the initiative quickly. The reader should bear in mind that this game was played at a relatively fast rate in a "marathon tournament" with twelve games in one weekend.

I felt that the sacrificial motif with 13 d4!? was very promising and akin to Kasparov's pawn sacrifice as Black in the Taimanov Variation against Karpov (See Taimanov,

Game 1). My play was very thematic and inspired right to the end.

1 e4 c5 2 ♘c3 ♘c6 3 g3 g6 4 ♗g2 ♗g7 5 d3 d6 6 f4 e6 7 ♘f3 ♘ge7

My favourite "Anti-Closed Sicilian Setup".

8 0-0 ♖b8 9 ♘e2 0-0 10 c3 b6

...♖b8 was played to support ...b5, but here I decided it was more important to concern myself with the activity of my queen's bishop, especially after White plays d4.

11 ♗e3 d5 12 e5 ♗a6 13 ♖e1

13...d4!?

A thematic "sweeper-sealer twist", opening up the d5 square while closing down White's d4. In return for a pawn Black suddenly becomes very active.

14 cxd4 ♘b4

Black hits d3 but also threatens ...♘f5 and ...♘d5. Here I recommend ♘c1 for White.

15 dxc5 ♘xd3 16 cxb6 ♖xb6!

Black eliminates a dangerous pawn; if 17 ♗xb6 ♕xb6 18 ♘fd4 ♘f5 and Black is winning.

17 b3 ♘f5 18 ♗f2 ♕c7

Black threatens to win by ...♘xf2 and ...♕c5+.

19 g4 ♘xf2 20 ♔xf2

20...Rd6!

This was a big surprise for White.

21 exd6 Wb6+ 22 ∆ed4 ∆xd4 23 ∆xd4 Bxd4+ 24 Kg3 Rd8!

Black could also play ...Bf2+ first.

25 Wf3 Bxa1 26 Rxa1 Wxd6

To control the d-file.

27 Re1 Wd2

Black has a won game now.

28 Wf2 Rd3+ 29 Bf3 Wc3 30 Kg2 Rxf3 31 Wxf3 Wxe1 32 h4 We2+ 0-1

Closed Sicilian (Game 7)
M.Ruiz-D.Kopec
Southern New England Open 1994

In this game, the "Anti-Closed" setup again works well for Black. White makes the mistake of trying to hold Black off in the sector of the board where Black is assured of an initiative in any case.

1 e4 c5 2 ∆f3 ∆c6 3 d3 g6 4 g3 Bg7 5 Bg2 e6 6 0-0 ∆ge7 7 ∆bd2 0-0 8 We2 d6 9 c3 b5 10 a3 Rb8 11 ∆e1 a5 12 f4 b4 13 axb4 axb4 14 ∆b1 bxc3 15 bxc3 ∆d4 16 Wd1 ∆b3 17 Ra3 ∆xc1 18 Wxc1 d5 19 e5 ∆f5 20 g4 ∆h4 21 Bh1 g5!

A timely lever to destroy White's centre.

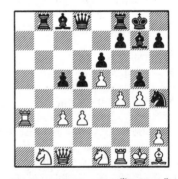

22 d4 cxd4 23 cxd4 Wb6 24 ∆c2 Ba6 25 Re1 gxf4 26 Wxf4 Wxb1 27 Rxb1 Rxb1+ 28 Kf2 Rf1+ 29 Kg3 Rxf4 30 Kxf4 Bc4 31 g5 ∆f5 32 Bf3 h6 0-1

B. The Grand Prix Attack

For a while, in the 1980s, this opening system with an early f4 against the Sicilian was a big point scorer for White, highlighted by the successes of the English Grandmaster Mark Hebden on the Grand Prix Circuit in England, from which it got its name.

But I still don't believe it! Maybe the system should score a few points for White due to its element of surprise, but with sound central counterattacking play, backed up by good development, Black should fare well.

Grand Prix Attack (Game 1)
J. Johnson-D.Kopec
Stratton Mountain Open 1993

The following game of mine, against a player who likes to attack, sums up my strong feelings about how Black should deal with quick-fire attempts at "driving Black off the board". The reader should also know that this was by no means the first time that I had faced the Grand Prix Attack—just the first time in a long time.

1 e4 c5 2 ♘c3 ♘c6 3 f4 g6 4 ♘f3 ♗g7 5 ♗c4 e6 6 f5 ♘ge7
This is considered Black's best setup. One important point, however: do not even think about capturing on f5—it is quite simply bad!

7 fxe6 dxe6
This is my preferred recapture, but theory actually favours ...fxe6. For an example of how play should then proceed, see Grand Prix Attack Game 2 below.

8 0-0 a6 9 a4 0-0 10 d3 ♘d4

Black immediately begins central counterplay. Exchanges should be helpful in neutralising White's plans for a kingside attack.

11 ♗g5 f6 12 ♗h4 ♘ec6
Black announces his intention to play solidly in the centre.

13 ♘xd4 cxd4 14 ♘e2 ♔h8

Black unpins his e-pawn and prepares to develop a central pawn chain with ...e5. Then Black, after completing his development, and trading off White's ♗c4 with ♕e2 and ♗e6, hopes to develop counterplay on the half-open c-file in traditional Sicilian fashion.

15 c3? dxc3
However White is impatient and facilitates Black's counterplay by weakening his pawn structure.

16 bxc3 ♘e5 17 ♕b3 ♘xc4 18 ♕xc4 e5
Black's two bishops—and two pawn islands to White's three—must spell an advantage. Notice how White's pieces (♘e2 and ♗h4) are not very effective.

19 ♖ab1 ♗g4 20 ♘c1 ♖c8 21 ♕b3 ♕d6 22 h3 ♗e6 23 ♕b6 ♕d7 24 c4 ♖f7 25 ♔h2 f5
Black has a significant advantage, although he only won after giving White lots of counterchances.

Grand Prix Attack (Game 2)
L.Braun-R.Blumenfeld
New York, 1989

The following game also illustrates typical play against the Grand Prix Attack. The player of the white pieces was one of the most active players in the USA in the 1980s— the late and much beloved, Leslie Braun. Playing Black is a strong Senior Master, Rudy Blumenfeld.

1 e4 c5 2 ♘c3 ♘c6 3 f4 g6 4 ♘f3 ♗g7 5 ♗c4 e6 6 f5 ♘ge7 7 fxe6 dxe6 8 d3 0-0 9 0-0 ♘a5

This theoretical jaunt is aimed at immediately obtaining the bishop-pair for Black.

10 ♗b3 ♘xb3 11 axb3 ♘c6 12 ♘e2 e5

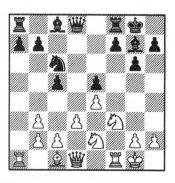

With two bishops and no squares for White's knights to aim for in the centre, Black can vie for an advantage.

13 ♗e3 ♘d4 14 ♘exd4 cxd4 15 ♗g5 f6 16 ♗d2

We have the same pawn structure which occurred in the previous game: Blumenfeld and I have

collaborated on some writing, but we have never consulted about this!

16...♗e6 17 ♖a4 ♕c7 18 ♕b1 a6 19 ♖c1 h6 20 ♔h1 ♕d7 21 c4

Blumenfeld now decides to shift his attention to the mobilization of his kingside pawn majority.

21...♗g4 22 ♖f1 f5 23 ♕e1 f4

Here I might have played 23...♖ae8, hoping to follow with ...fxe4, but Black has a more deliberate approach.

24 ♖a5 ♖ae8 25 b4 g5 26 b5 axb5 27 ♖xb5 ♗h5 28 ♕d1 ♗f6

Blumenfeld, who is quite familiar with King's Indian Defence attacks, completes final preparations for a pawn storm.

29 ♕b3 ♖f7 30 ♗e1 ♔h8 31 ♖d5 ♕c8 32 ♕b5 ♗xf3 33 ♖xf3 h5

Methodically advancing on the kingside.

34 ♖f1 h4 35 ♗b4 g4 36 ♗d2 ♗g7 37 ♗a5 ♔h7 38 ♗b6 f3 39 ♕c5 fxg2+ 40 ♔xg2 h3+ 41 ♔g1 ♖xf1+ 42 ♔xf1 ♕e6

And now he is shifting to a decisive infiltration.

43 ♗c7 ♕f7+ 44 ♔e1 ♖c8 0-1

Grand Prix Attack (Game 3)
E.Pinter-J.Banas
Nove Zamky, 1999

The following game illustrates the virtues of the more thematic recapture by Black, 7...fxe6, in the Grand Prix Attack. It also shows the consequences of not adhering to the principles of sound opening play. With a few pawn sacrifices to open lines and increase the range of his light-squared bishop, Black finds ways of menacing the white king, caught in the centre.

1 e4 c5 2 ♘c3 ♘c6 3 f4 g6 4 ♘f3 ♗g7 5 ♗c4 e6 6 f5 ♘ge7 7 fxe6 fxe6 8 d3 d5 9 ♗b3 b5

Quite a sharp move which is thematic to Black's counterplay.

10 a3 c4 11 ♗a2 b4!?

Quite direct but a bit impetuous. Black has a certain pawn sacrifice in mind. He could also play ...0-0 or ...♕b6

12 axb4 ♘xb4 13 dxc4 ♘xa2 14 ♖xa2 d4 15 ♘e2 e5

This is Black's theme. At the expense of a pawn he gains a strong centre, two bishops and play against the isolated white e-pawn.

16 ♗g5 ♗b7 17 ♘d2 0-0 18 ♘c1

White will not be able to castle.

18...♕c7 19 ♘d3 a5 20 ♕e2 ♘c8 21 c5 ♗a6 22 ♖f1 ♖xf1+ 23 ♕xf1 ♘a7

24 ♕f3 ♘c6 25 ♖a3 ♖f8 26 ♕h3 ♕f7

Black threatens ...♗xd3 and ...♕f2+ etc.

27 ♘f3 ♕c4 28 ♔d1 ♘b4 29 ♘xb4 axb4 30 ♖d3 b3

Exploiting the overworked pawn on c2 to open lines.

31 ♖xb3 ♕e2+ 32 ♔c1 ♗c8

If now 33 g4? h5 is very nasty.

33 ♕h4 ♕xg2 34 ♕g3 ♕f1+ 35 ♔d2 ♗e6 36 ♗e7 ♗h6+ 0-1

White loses a rook or gets mated.

C. The c3 Variation

I have never felt any reason to fear the "c3 Variation" against the Sicilian Defence. Again, White neglects development in an attempt to construct a strong centre. I believe that if White is going to do this, he might as well first improve his development with 2 ♘f3 and only then play 3 ♗d3 followed by c3 (The Kopec System!).

Closed Sicilian (Game 1)
J.Sanz-D.Kopec
Aaronson Masters London 1978

1 e4 c5 2 c3 ♘f6
I believe this is Black's soundest move, leading to the gain of the d5 square (essentially for ever!), but Black has also had little trouble equalizing with 2...d5. The trouble with the latter move is that White has an array of systems at his disposal.
3 e5 ♘d5 4 d4 cxd4 5 cxd4 d6 6 ♘f3 ♘c6 7 ♗c4
Now the thematic move is 7...♘b6, but I have demonstrated that the text move, 7...e6, is quite playable too.
7...e6 8 0-0 ♗e7 9 ♕e2 0-0 10 ♘c3 ♘xc3 11 bxc3
Now Black has a backward pawn on c3 as a target.
11...d5 12 ♗d3 ♘a5 13 ♕c2
As is typical in the c3 Sicilian, White tries to force play on the kingside, but this costs time...
13...h6 14 ♗f4 ♗d7 15 ♕c1 g5!

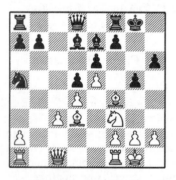

...which is why I think I can and should play this move. Black's weakened kingside is offset by his gain of time.
16 ♗b1 ♔g7
Black constructs a viable defence for his exposed king.
17 ♗e3 ♖h8 18 ♗d3 ♖c8 19 ♖b1 b6 20 ♗a6 ♖b8 21 ♗d3 ♖c8 22 ♗a6 ♖b8 23 ♗d3 ♕c7
I decided to play for a win!
24 ♘d2 b5 25 f4 ♖bc8 26 ♗xb5 ♕xc3 27 ♕xc3 ♖xc3 28 ♗xd7 ♖xe3
Now, while White is getting into severe time pressure, Black tries to find a focal point for his counter-attack. It turns out that the white pawn on d4 is the most vulnerable one in the position.
29 f5 exf5 30 ♗xf5 ♖a3 31 ♖b2 ♗d8

The beginning of the end for White.
32 ♘f3 ♗b6 33 ♖e2 ♘c6 34 ♖d1 ♘e7 35 ♗d7 ♖d8 36 e6 fxe6 37 ♗xe6 ♘c6 38 ♗g4 ♖a4 39 ♖ed2 ♔g6 40 ♔f1 h5 41 ♖c1 ♖c4 42 ♖xc4 dxc4 43 ♗e6 g4 44 ♘h4+ ♔g5 45 g3 c3 0-1
All of Black's pieces coordinated well in the end.

c3 Sicilian (Game 2)
Aaronson Masters. London 1979
M.Chandler-D.Kopec

In the following gamelet we will see Black once again equalizing by very direct means, although later he did blunder and lose.

1 e4 c5 2 c3 ♘f6 3 e5 ♘d5 4 d4 cxd4 5 ♘f3 ♘c6 6 cxd4 d6 7 ♗c4 e6 8 0-0 ♗e7 9 a3 0-0 10 ♕e2 ♕b6 11 ♖d1 dxe5 12 dxe5 ♖d8 13 ♕e4 ♘a5 14 ♘bd2 ♗d7 15 ♗d3 g6 16 ♘c4 ♘xc4 17 ♗xc4 ♗a4 18 ♖e1 ♗c6 19 ♗g5 ♘c7 20 ♕f4 ♗xf3 21 ♗xe7 ♖d4 22 ♕xf3 ♖xc4 23 b3 ♖c2 24 ♖ac1 ♖xc1 25 ♖xc1 ♘d5 26 ♗d6 ♕d8 27 ♖c2 h5 28 h3 ♖c8

The game is equal.

D. The Kopec System

For more than thirty years and over several hundred games, I have developed a system for White against the Sicilian Defence which starts out 1 e4 c5 2 ♘f3 d6/♘c6/e6 3 ♗d3!? This system has scored many points for me. The idea is that White develops quickly and castles, but must also play c3 followed by ♗c2 in order to threaten d4. It leads

the sharp Sicilian player into a positional type of struggle, not unlike the Ruy Lopez.

Black has naturally tried many setups against the Kopec System—the most solid and difficult of which is undoubtedly the "Russian setup": ...c5, ...d6, ...e5, ...g6, in conjunction with ...♘c6, ...♘ge7, and ...♗g7, against which it is very difficult for White to gain an advantage. One game of mine against GM Alexander Ivanov went:

D.Kopec-A.Ivanov
13th Queen City Open 1989

1 e4

This turned out to be the first of three consecutive years that GM Alexander Ivanov and I met in the same tournament in the same round (4)—the Queen City Open in Manchester, New Hampshire. I can't say I'm unhappy with the score of those encounters: 2½-½ in my favour, including two Kopec System games!

1...c5 2 ♘f3 d6 3 ♗d3 ♘c6 4 c3 g6 5 0-0 ♗g7 6 ♗c2 e5 7 d3 ♘ge7 8 h3 h6 9 ♗e3 f5 10 exf5 ♗xf5

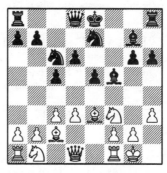

Exactly one year later Ivanov played 10...gxf5, following my recommendation. He did gain an advantage, but then played inaccurately and I eventually salvaged a draw in time pressure.

E. Closed Systems with ♗b5

Black need not fear positions resulting from ♗b5 on move 3, 4, or 5 by White. In many cases Black should, however, be careful to avoid the tempo-losing ...a6, since White is likely to capture on c6 anyway. Often a better challenge to the bishop is to play ...♘d4. One game I played as White, against IM Jean Hébert in Montreal 1978, went 1 e4 c5 2 ♘f3 e6 3 ♘c3 ♘c6 4 ♗b5 ♘d4! and now I fell into the trap 5 ♘xd4? (better 5 a4) cxd4 6 ♘e2 ♕g5! 7 ♘xd4? ♕c5 8 c3 e5 and White lost a piece for insufficient compensation.

♗b5 System (Game 1)
S.Zeidler-D.Kopec
4NCL, England 1998

The following game shows how Black, by typically sound and solid play coupled with a timely counterattack, can score a resounding victory against systems where White plays an early ♗b5.

1 e4 c5 2 ♘c3 ♘c6 3 ♗b5 ♘d4 4 ♗c4 e6

White's bishop is blunted.

5 ♘ge2 ♘e7 6 0-0 a6 7 a4 d5 8 exd5 exd5

Black already grabs a lion's share of the centre.

9 ♘xd4 dxc4

Black avoids 9...cxd4 10 ♘xd5 ♘xd5 11 ♕h5 ♗e6 12 ♖e1 which, although not fully clear, does seem unpleasant for Black.

10 ♘f3 ♘c6

Black proceeds solidly. The doubled black c-pawns have a cramping effect on White's position.

11 ♘e4 ♗e7 12 ♖a3 ♗g4 13 h3 ♗xf3 14 ♖xf3 0-0 15 ♖e1 f5

Fully developed, Black begins his counterattack, based on his control of the centre and fluid development.

16 ♘g3 ♘d4 17 ♖a3 f4 18 ♘e2 ♘c6

A move I was proud of since it emphasizes the simple soundness of Black's position. Although he finds it difficult, White must try to advance his b, c, or d-pawns.

19 d3 f3 20 ♘f4 fxg2 21 ♘e6 ♕d7 22 ♕g4 ♖f7 23 dxc4 ♗f6 24 ♘xc5?

Black finds a simple refutation of this grab. In any case he stands better.

24...♕xg4 25 hxg4 ♗e7 26 ♖xe7 ♖xe7 27 ♗e3

White's position would just about hang together were it not for Black's next move.

27...♘e5! 28 ♖b3 ♘xc4 29 ♗d4

Not 29 ♖xb7 ♖xb7 30 ♘xb7 ♖b8 31 ♘c5 ♘xe3 32 fxe3 ♖xb2 33 ♘xa6 ♖xc2 and Black wins.

29...b6 30 ♘d3 ♘d2 0-1

White will soon be at least a rook down.

Closed System with ♗g5 (Game 2)
J.Berry-D.Kopec
London International 1997

I'll finish with a game against an old friend, Jonathan Berry, who exacted revenge for a win I scored against him nearly 30 years earlier when we were both 15—in Yakima, Washington. However I think that this game still holds as an excellent example of how Black should play in these "Closed Systems". It's a shame I blundered in Berry's time pressure—trying to be too smart with 27 ♘d5??.

1 e4 c5 2 f4 ♘c6 3 ♘f3 g6 4 ♗b5 ♘d4 5 ♘xd4 cxd4 6 0-0 ♕b6 7 ♘a3 e6 8 ♗a4 a6 9 d3 ♕c7 10 ♗d2 b5 11 ♗b3 ♗g7 12 ♔h1 ♘e7 13 c3 dxc3 14 ♗xc3 ♗xc3 15 ♖c1 ♗b7 16 ♖xc3 ♕b6 17 ♕e1 f5 18 ♖c2 0-0 19 ♖e2 ♕d4 20 ♖f3 ♖ac8 21 h3 ♖f7

Actually the resemblence between this position and the one which occurred in Orlov-Taimanov (Chapter 5) after 27 ♖f7 is quite striking.

22 ♔h2 ♔g7 23 g4 fxe4 24 dxe4 ♖cf8 25 ♘c2 ♕d6 26 ♕c3+ ♔g8

Amazingly, the right move seems to be 26...♔h6!

27 ♖d2 ♘d5??

27...♕c6 was still winning.

28 exd5 ♖xf4 29 dxe6 ♖d4+ 30 ♔g1 ♖xf3 31 e7+ 1-0

Index of Games

Abayasakera-Kopec	14	Matulović-Fischer	7
Adams-Kasparov	114	McKay-Kopec	20
Anand-Kasparov	1, 49, 52, 54	Minić-Fischer	83
Barrios-Kopec	71	Nokes-Kopec	37
Beliavsky-Georgiev	55	Orlov-Taimanov	104
Berry-Kopec	127	Peters-Kopec	29
Braun-Blumenfeld	122	Pinter-Banas	123
Browne-Kopec	21	Polgar-Taimanov	106
Chandler-Kopec	125	Pritchett-Soltis	47
Drexel-Kopec	30	Rauzer-Botvinnik	35
Enders-Kramnik	58	Ruiz-Kopec	120
Farkas-Zagrebelny	114	Saint Amant-Staunton	111
Fernandes-Limp	64	Sanguinetti-Fischer	80
Fischer-Spassky	72, 74	Sanz-Kopec	124
Fischer-Tal	78, 108	Schneider-Kopec	31
Fichtl-Malich	19	Seidler-Kopec	26
Gallagher-Dizdarević	101	Short-Kasparov	85, 88
Gilden-Kopec	41	Short-Leko	116
Howe-Kopec	119	Short-Topalov	46
Hübner-Anand	93	Smyslov-Botvinnik	111, 112
Ivanov-Kopec	25	Spassky-Fischer	81, 86
Iversland-Kopec	41	Spassky-Mestel	48
Jansa-Babula	67	Stewart-Kopec	26
Johnson-Kopec	121	Stripunsky-Kopec	73
Liberzon-Miles	50	Suetin-Szabo	33
Kalesis-Kotronias	68	Tiviakov-Miezes	100, 101
Karpov-Kasparov	15, 103	Tiviakov-Milov	100
Karpov-Korchnoi	44	Topalov-Kasparov	23
Karpov-Taimanov	107	Unzicker-Fischer	92
Kasparov-Gelfand	90	Vasiescu-Andrescu	60
Kornev-Belikov	65	Velimirović-Ljubojević	82
Kosashvili-Greenfeld	95	Velimirović-Hazzar	82
Lane-Kopec	117	Wells-Kozul	61
London-Kopec	42	Wolff-Kopec	39
Luther-Hraček	70	Wostyn-Sax	13
Mamadshoev-Nijboer	100	Ziatdinov-Gurevich	63